The Hedgehog Primer

by Antigone M. Means-Burleson, Ph.D.

Copyright © 2003, Antigone Means-Burleson, Ph.D.
All rights reserved.
No part of this book may be reproduced, stored in a retrieval system, or transmitted by any means, electronic, mechanical, photocopying, recording, or otherwise, without written permission from the author.
Published by Instantpublisher.com
International Standard Book Number: 1-59196-211-0

Table of Contents

I. An introduction to hedgehogs
    A. What kind of animal is a hedgehog?
    B. What species are these hedgehogs?
    C. The history of hedgehogs in the pet trade
    D. Are hedgehogs good pets?
    E. Where do I find a hedgehog?
    F. Why are hedgehogs expensive?
    G. How do I choose a pet hedgehog?
        1. Gender differences
        2. Temperament
        3. Health
II. Getting ready for a pet hedgehog
    A. Housing
    B. Environment
    C. Feeding
    D. Exercise
    E. Bedding
    F. Cage accessories and toys
    G. Check your attitude and expectations
    H. Finding a veterinarian
    I. Finding the right hedgehog for you

III. When hedgehog comes home
    A. Handling hedgehogs
    B. Common adjustment difficulties
    C. Understanding behavior/communication
    D. Behavioral issues
        1. Biting
        2. Quilling
        3. Self-anointing
    E. Hedgehog hide and seek ("hedgie-proofing")

IV. Keeping your hedgehog healthy
    A. When to take your hedgehog to the vet
    B. Common medical problems
        1. Mites
        2. Respiratory infections
        3. Tumors and abscesses
        4. Fatty liver
        5. Dental issues
        6. Obesity
        7. Ear problems
        8. "Wobbliness"
        9. Fleas
    C. Cleanliness and bathing
    D. Communicating with your veterinarian
    E. What to keep in your hedgehog care/first aid kit

V. Beyond the basics
    A. Travel with hedgehogs
    B. Hedgehogs and other pets
    C. Hedgehogs in public settings
    D. Hedgehog colors
    E. The hedgehog community
        1. International Hedgehog Association
        2. Showing your hedgehog
        3. Online communities
    F. Preparing for a pet sitter

VI. Breeding hedgehogs
    A. Introduction to the perils of breeding
    B. Licensure
    C. The many hats of a hedgehog breeder
    D. Breeder ethics
    E. From beginning to babies
        1. Choosing breeding stock
        2. Putting them together
        3. Pregnancy
        4. Infancy
        5. Toddlerhood
        5. Weaning

      F. Hand feeding
      G. Predicting adult color from baby color
VII. Making things for your hedgehog
      A. Hedgebag
      B. Craft foam tubes
      C. Storage tote cage
      D. Fleece blanket
      E. Storage blocks playpen
      G. Toys from "trash"
VIII. Resources
      A. Bibliography
      B. Recommended Readings
      C. Internet Resources
IX. Index
X. Apendices
      A. Hedgehog's Journal
      B. Additional Photos
      C. Acknowledgements

Chapter 1: An Introduction To Hedgehogs

What is a hedgehog?

Hedgehogs are small mammals with prickly tops, furry bellies, and adorable little faces that have captured the hearts of many since their initial introduction to the pet world in the early 1990s. Since that time, hedgehogs have gone from virtually unknown to being well-loved family members in thousands of homes in North America, South America, Europe, and Asia. Despite their growing popularity, quality care information about hedgehogs has been hard to come by and a quick search of the Internet will make it clear that conflicting views abound. This book is based on my experience with pet hedgehogs since 1995, with breeding hedgehogs since 1996, and showing and judging hedgehogs since 1997. The information in this book should give you all of the basics that you need to know in order to keep your hedgehog happy and healthy!

What species are these hedgehogs?

Hedgehogs belong to the insectivore class, along with their distant cousins the tenrec, shrews, and moon rats. The hedgehogs that are typically kept as pets in North America are referred to as "African Pygmy Hedgehogs." The term pygmy is a misnomer as these hedgehogs are not truly pygmies, just small in comparison to the widely-known European hedgehog. Size can range from as little as 6 ounces to as much as 32 ounces, though most will weigh between 12 ounces and 18 ounces. This puts them at somewhere between the size of a baseball and soft ball.

Many people are surprised to discover that the hedgehog is not at all related to the porcupine. Porcupines are rodents and in the order Rodentia, and their quills are barbed, hollow, and only lightly attached. Hedgehogs belong to the order Insectivora, which includes only hedgehogs, tenrec, shrews, and gymnure (mole rats). Hedgehog quills are also hollow, but the resemblance ends there. Hedgehog quills are not barbed and remain attached to serve as a very different sort of defense than is exhibited by the porcupine.

Sometimes the hedgehog is confused with the North American groundhog (also known as a marmot or woodchuck). Unfortunately, African hedgehogs have been released into the wild by negligent pet owners, but North American and European climates become too cold in the winter and it is unlikely that any would survive. If someone in North America says they saw a fast-moving hedgehog in their yard, it is most likely that they are actually describing a groundhog and have the two mixed up.

African hedgehogs of the White Bellied (Atelerix albiventris) and Algerian (Atelerix algirus) species were imported to the United States after they were allegedly discovered by a pet importer on a collection trip to Nigeria, around 1990. At this point in time, most hedgehogs in the North American pet trade are a hybrid of these two species, since they successfully interbred before anyone realized that they represented similar but different species. The long-eared desert hedgehogs (Hemiechinus auritus) were also imported into the United States, but the general consensus of persons who had them was that their temperament was not as even and they did not breed as readily as the Atelerix and are now generally not available in North America. Other species, such as long-eared desert hedgehogs are kept as pets outside of North America, but they are not readily available here and my experience with them is limited, so this book will refer to the type that are of the White Bellied, Algerian, or a hybrid of the two.

The oral history recounts that the original importer was presented with the hedgehogs, a pest in their native region, which were sold to him for fifty cents each. It is purported that he shipped several thousand to the United States. Initially, these hedgehogs sold for hundreds to thousands of dollars each as people hoped to get rich with the next "in" pet. The boom was fueled by a USDA ban on the importation of hedgehogs around 1993, due to hedgehogs' potential as a vector for the hoof and mouth disease that occurs in their native lands. This fad market quickly dropped out as people realized that no one was going to get rich on hedgehogs. In its place, a solid community of persons interested in maintaining and improving the quality of the species in captivity has evolved. In the mid to late '90's, there were many hobby breeders who sold them to individuals and pet stores. When the price of pet hedgehogs dropped and the USDA stepped in to regulate the sales of pocket pets, many of these hobby breeders discontinued.

Are hedgehogs good pets?

Whether or not a hedgehog makes a good pet depends upon two things- the hedgehog and the person. Hedgehogs are partially domesticated at this point, but the fact remains that they are basically wild animals, with a lot of wild instincts. A hedgehog can not be expected to be readily trained to meet human expectations, so it is very important to examine one's own expectations and look for a hedgehog that will be a good match. It is also very important to have realistic expectations. Here is a list of things that you can expect from a hedgehog:

- Hedgehogs are largely nocturnal, or may be considered somewhat crepuscular (awake at twilight and midnight) and will generally prefer to be awake at night, rather than during the day. They may make some noise as they go about their business at night They do not bark, chirp, or squeak but may bang their cage furnishings about.
- You will get prickled. Even the friendliest hedgehogs have their off moments and many will react to strange sounds, fast movement, or other unfamiliar situations by raising their quills or rolling in a tight ball.
- Your hedgehog will need to stay warm. They are desert creatures and are not meant to hibernate. If kept at too cool of temperatures, they can get sick and die.
- Hedgehogs can bite. It is not their usual defense, but anything with teeth can bite.

- Your hedgehog will need its cage cleaned at least once or twice per week, depending on the type of bedding that you choose. Some bedding, such as vellux or plain newsprint, will need to be changed daily.
- Your hedgehog will need fresh food and water daily. The water bottle may leak, or the hedgehog may soil its food. For this reason, you can not simply fill up the food dish and water bottle and leave your hedgehog for several days.
- Your hedgehog will probably need to see the veterinarian at least once in its lifetime. Not all veterinarians have experience with or will see hedgehogs, so you will need to find a qualified veterinarian before it becomes an issue.
- You can expect that your hedgehog will live an average of 3 to 6 years. Just like humans and other pets, some may live short lives while others live beyond this expectancy.
- Your hedgehog does not need another hedgehog as a companion. Some females may accept or even enjoy a companion, but males generally will not.
- You will need to spend at least a little time, and sometimes a lot of time, daily with your hedgehog if you want it to become used to your sound, smell, and touch.
- If you are afraid of your hedgehog, it will probably make the hedgehog nervous.
- Hedgehogs each have their own personalities and not all will want to interact with you in the same way.
- Your hedgehog may eliminate on you, especially if it is very young or very old.
- Your hedgehog may never actively seek you out for companionship. Some hedgehogs do, but most just think humans are cool terrain to climb on.
- Most babies will go through a period of "quilling" and will be very grumpy for a while. This can last for several months. You will need to hold it anyway, if you want to keep it from learning that this is a good way to get people to leave it alone.
- Hedgehogs may not be legal where you live. At the time of this printing, it is illegal to have a hedgehog in California, Arizona, Vermont, Hawaii, Pennsylvania, Georgia, and Maine. It is also illegal to own hedgehog in some cities or counties. If you own a hedgehog illegally, you may face fines and the confiscation and euthanization of your hedgehog if it comes to the attention of the authorities.
- While hedgehogs are well tolerated by many persons with allergies, there is no guarantee that they will be tolerated by all. Persons who are allergic to wood beddings will typically experience an allergic reaction when handling hedgehogs due to minute amounts of it secreted into the skin when poked by quills.
- Hedgehogs do not have a strong body odor like domestic mice, rats, and ferrets but they still eliminate waste and someone with a very sensitive nose can still smell a hedgehog.
- Hedgehogs love to explore and hide so you an not leave a hedgehog unattended without "hedgie proofing" your home. Check out the Hedgehog Hide and Seek section for more information.
- While many hedgehogs do use a litter box, your hedgehog may be one that does not.
- Hedgehogs have a propensity toward obesity and you may need to monitor your hedgehog's diet carefully. As insectivores, they require some attention to diet to meet their special needs, though they do not require to eat live insects to stay healthy.

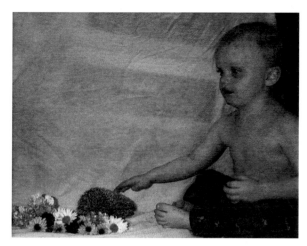

1a. Whether a hedgehog makes a good pet depends both upon the hedgehog and the individual. Here, a toddler makes friends with a hedgehog.

In short, hedgehogs are an unusual and interesting animal, but they are not for everybody. If you are caring, flexible, observant, able to meet its care needs, and able to accept your hedgehog for what it is, rather than what you want it to be, then a hedgehog may be a good pet for you. Many people wonder if a hedgehog would make a good pet for a child and the answer is the same as for an adult- a definite maybe. If you are considering a hedgehog for a child's pet, please think about all of these considerations in terms of the child and also remember that ultimately, the adult must take final responsibility for the pet.

Where do I find a hedgehog?

If all of the cautions haven't scared you off, the next thing to consider is where to find a pet hedgehog. The main choices that are available are from a pet store, from a person who no longer wants theirs, or from a breeder. There are advantages and disadvantages to each of these choices. The advantage of purchasing from a pet store is that you can see the hedgehog, handle it, and decide if it's what you want. The disadvantage is that pet stores typically have no background information on the animal, may not give correct information on its age or care requirements, have quite limited guarantees, and are generally not able to provide follow-up care. In addition, many pet shops keep their hedgehogs in mixed-sex groups and the females may be pregnant when purchased. Many pet stores in the US are unaware that they require a USDA license and may obtain their animals from breeders who are similarly unlicensed and who may engage in substandard breeding practices, in order to be able to produce hedgehogs cheaply enough for mass sales.

Obtaining a hedgehog from a person who can no longer keep it, which includes adopting from a rescue organization, has pros and cons as well. Quite often, these hedgehogs are adults so you do not have to deal with quilling and the personality will be apparent. If you are adopting from an individual, they may not be able to provide much accurate information or any follow-up. Most rescue organizations can give good care information and follow-up assistance. The down side is that as an adult, it may have less lifespan to spend with you and may have experienced substandard care earlier in its life. There may be health or temperament issues that prompted its placement in a new home, so you will need to consider these issues carefully.

Purchasing from a breeder is also a mixed bag. Breeders come with different levels of expertise and quality, so you will need to be very careful to ask lots of questions and make sure that you are comfortable that what you are getting is what you want. Potential advantages of purchasing from a breeder include knowledge about the hedgehog's background, experience, health guarantees that may be better than those available elsewhere, knowledge and hedgehog-specific experience, follow-up care, and the availability of specific information about the individual hedgehog. The down side is that purchasing from a breeder is no guarantee of quality and the buyer must beware. The other disadvantage may be that shipping can be expensive if you do not have a quality breeder who lives close by. The only way to legally ship a hedgehog is via air freight or by licensed van lines, so you should be very alarmed if a breeder offers to ship you a hedgehog by an overnight door-to-door postal service. This is both illegal and highly dangerous for the hedgehog. Do not be afraid to ask the breeder a lot of questions or to ask for references. Quality breeders will appreciate your effort to make an informed decision.

Why are hedgehogs expensive?

Anyone who has priced hedgehogs will quickly recognize that they are much more expensive than common small animals, such as rabbits, hamsters, and guinea pigs. There are several reasons for this. First, hedgehogs are slow to reproduce. While a hamster can have babies once a month, a female hedgehog may only have babies 2 or 3 times a year. Hedgehogs average 3 to 4 babies per litter, with an infant mortality rate of about 33%. Hedgehog females only have an optimal breeding span of 1-1/2 to 2 years, as compared to their lifespan of 3 to 6 years. This means that an average female produces

1b. Hedgehogs typically have three to four babies per litter.

approximately 7 to 14 babies in her lifetime, less than a tenth of the babies possible to an average rodent female. Feeding a quality diet, providing good veterinary care, and maintaining USDA licensure create substantial expenses for breeders, who cannot offset these expenses by sheer numbers as can be done with animals that reproduce quickly.

How do I choose a pet hedgehog?

Regardless of where you decide to obtain your hedgehog, the same criteria will apply in making your choice. The three biggest things to consider will be gender differences, temperament, and health. Many people also consider the hedgehog's color, but that is more a matter of personal preference than the other considerations. Age is also a consideration. If you are purchasing a baby, make sure that your baby is at least 6 weeks old. Hedgehogs typically wean to hard food at about 5 weeks old and your baby will need at least a week of eating and drinking on its own to make sure that it is well established on its own. Hedgehogs are considered fully adult at approximately 6 months of age.

Gender differences

Many people are convinced that female animals are naturally friendlier than males. This is just not the case with hedgehogs. After handling hundreds of hedgehogs, it has definitely been my experience that there are no consistent differences between how male and female hedgehogs interact with human beings. That does not mean that there are not other gender differences.

The first thing to consider is that males and females do differ in how they react to other hedgehogs. Males tend to be more territorial than females will often attack or kill another male cage mate, even if they seem to get along at first. A male cannot be kept with a female cage mate because the result will be babies. More often than not they will eat the babies if she delivers while they are still together. Male hedgehogs have internal genitalia that make neutering a risky procedure, so it is not recommended to pursue neutering for the express purpose of being able to house a male and female together. Most, but not all, females will accept a cage mate and some even prefer having a companion. So, the general rule here is that if you want one hedgehog, get a male. If you want to house more than one together, get females.

The second thing to consider is health related. There is a growing body of evidence that suggests that unbred females have an increased risk of reproductive problems, such as pyometria and uterine cancer. Because spaying is an expensive, complicated, and somewhat risky procedure in hedgehogs, preventive spaying is not widely recommended. Instead, persons who own female hedgehogs are encouraged to have regular veterinary check ups and to be prepared for the expense should reproductive problems occur. The rate of recovery with early intervention is encouraging. While reproductive problems are not as frequent in males, they do need to be monitored for irritations to their penile sheath. Since their penis elongates from their body when they urinate and they are relatively close to the ground, some types of bedding may be drawn back into the penile sheath.

Before departing from this topic area, it is important to note the physical characteristics that distinguish males and females. To determine gender, you must be able to get a good look at your hedgehog's underbelly. Females have a very small urogenital gap while males have a large gap. The placement of the penile sheath gives males the appearance of having a belly button.

Temperament

Temperament is an extremely important consideration. It is absolutely unreasonable to expect that all hedgehogs will behave in the same way or that all hedgehogs will conform to behaving the way that the owner wants them to behave. Knowing what kind of personality you want in a hedgehog will help you to choose one that will be a better match for you. There are four basic hedgehog personality styles:

- Snugglers: These hedgehogs like to be held. Some will curl up at your neck, others like your lap or the crook of you arm. They are usually calm and content to be held quietly. They may also let you pick them up with spines completely down

- Scaredy cats: These hedgehogs may unball and snuggle or may explore, but it seems like the slightest thing scares them and they instantly snap into a ball at the tiniest noise or movement. They need a lot of patience and understanding, and with time may learn to be a runner or a snuggler, though most will always retain that high-strung tendency.

- <u>Runners</u>: These hedgehogs just don't want to sit still. They are perpetual motion machines, and squirm like crazy when you try and hold them in your hands. They do well with lots of things to climb on and under, and lots of room to roam. They usually think you're pretty neat to climb, and may want to sample your hair. They stay busy and are a lot of fun to watch or to let roam over you like terrain.

1c. Some hedgehogs are shy and easily startled. If you are nervous when handling a hedgehog, it may make the hedgehog even more nervous, so that it balls up like this one.

- <u>Hermits</u>: Some hedgehogs just want to be grumpy and hide, no matter what. They may be out and about comfortably, but run and hide or ball up the moment they notice a human is about. Some may even bite to let you know that they don't appreciate being handled. They typically have a feisty, fun spirit, but it takes some understanding and patience to learn how they want you to behave. They are not hedgehogs who will voluntarily seek you out, though they may learn to tolerate your presence.

If you think that one or more of these styles would not be a good match for you, then do not purchase a hedgehog that is clearly a poor match. Keep in mind that their personalities can change and it can be very difficult to tell what a baby hedgehog will be like when it grows up. They go through several phases where they can be cranky and sellers do not have a foolproof way to know which will remain grumpy and which will grow out of it. It is important to communicate with the seller about the baby's behavior and to be prepared to cope with temporary crankiness. Young hedgehogs who are reinforced for cranky behavior by being set down or avoided learn to continue this behavior, in order to keep away what they think of as potential predators (that means you). If you are nervous, it may affect your hedgehog's behavior, making even a friendly hedgehog nervous.

When you choose a hedgehog, it should unball so that you can see its face and it should at least partially lay its quills down without constantly huffing and clicking. Be cautious about buying a hedgehog that doesn't uncurl and "clicks" in addition to the scared huffing and popping. The clicking is potentially a sign of much more aggressive behavior.

Hedgehog temperament appears to result from a combination of genetics and socialization. Matching the environmental response to the hedgehog's needs will bring out the best in the individual hedgehog. An outgoing, friendly hedgehog can handle longer, noisier, more interactive handling sessions than a shy, anxious hedgehog. A shy, anxious hedgehog especially needs quiet, loving contact, or sometimes gentle talk and limited intrusion, to help bring out its best. It's important to remember that all hedgehogs are not the same, and the way that we treat them can help them to feel secure and happy in their home.

1d. It is a sign of good temperament when a hedgehog readily uncurls enough that you can see its face.

Keep in mind that the seller only knows what the hedgehog's behavior has been like in their environment and there is no way to guarantee that the hedgehog will maintain the same temperament in a different environment. Choosing a hedgehog that has the personality you like increases the chances that it will meet your expectations, but it is important to expect that hedgehogs, like all animals, are not totally predictable.

Health

The health of the hedgehog you are purchasing is also of utmost importance. There is no way to guarantee that any animal is free of hidden problems, but a good visual examination can identify some very obvious ones. You may also want to have your hedgehog visit a veterinarian for a well pet visit during the first 48 hours to make sure that you catch any problems that may be obvious to the vet and to give the vet an idea of what is normal for that hedgehog. Here are the things that you will need to check:
- <u>Clear eyes</u>: They should not be crusty, sunken, or swollen. The hedgehog should appear alert and aware.
- <u>Clean fur and quills</u>: The hedgehog's quills may not be perfectly clean (the lighter the hedgehog, the more they seem to like getting into stuff), but should not appear to be filthy all over. If there is fecal matter matted around the anal area, this is often a sign that the animal has diarrhea or some other problem that may indicate health problems.
- <u>Healthy skin</u>: Yellowing of the arm pits can be a sign of liver problems, particularly in adults. You will want to make sure that the skin is pink and clear. Mottled, dark

pigment can occur naturally and is not a concern. Skin can be dry for a variety of reasons. Gas heat can create a dry environment, resulting in dry skin. Some beddings, particularly wood beddings, can dry out the skin. However, dry skin can also be related to mites, fungus or nutritional deficits. Crustiness around the quills can be a sign that it isn't just dryness an may indicate a greater problem.

1e. With her bright eyes and alert demeanor, this little hedgehog appears nice and healthy.

- Scabs or injuries: If there are any, they should be healing well, and the seller should be able to tell you how they happened and what treatment has been given. For example, an ingrown quill that is healing nicely may not be an issue, but an ingrown quill with pus and some infection apparent probably is. As a prospective owner, you will want to consider the possible impact that injuries may have on your new pet so that you can decide if it is something you're prepared to manage.
- Groomed feet: Hedgehogs are notorious for what we call "poopy feet" so a little bit of this is to be expected. However, the hedgehog should not have nails that are overgrown and they should not be so dirty that you cannot inspect the feet. If the hedgehog needs its nails trimmed, ask the seller to show you how.
- Weight: The hedgehog should not be too fat (can't roll into a ball, has excess "bags" at the "armpit" areas) or too thin (hollow sides, caved looking tummy). Either can indicate poor health.
- Smell: The hedgehog should not have a foul odor. This is a sign that something is definitely wrong. Foul odor can indicate that it may have been kept in unsanitary conditions or may have some form of bacterial infection.
- Stool quality: Stools should be relatively firm and brownish in color. Green coloration or loose stools can occur under times of stress and may or may not indicate problems. Foods that use bright dyes can cause discoloration of the stool. If the stool is blackish and tarry this may signify major problems, while gelatinous stool may indicate bacterial imbalances or infections.

Giving the hedgehog a careful visual examination will help you catch a high percentage of health problems. If your hedgehog is being shipped to you, it is well worth the price of the veterinarian's health certificate to have your hedgehog examined prior to shipping.

A follow-up well pet visit at approximately two to four weeks after purchase will allow the vet to see if any problems have developed as the hedgehog has settled in. Ask the seller about health guarantees as some may offer replacement animals, some may assist with veterinary care should problems arise, and some simply offer the hedgehog as is. It should be expected that minor, stress-related problems, such as mites or gastrointestinal distress, are common during times of transition, so you will want to clarify what is your responsibility and what is the seller's. Knowing the policy ahead of time will eliminate a lot of disappointment and frustration for both you and the seller if problems do arise.

1f. A curious hedgehog out exploring!

Chapter 2: Getting ready for a pet hedgehog

Before you bring any new animal into your household, it is important to invest the time and money in preparation, so as to avoid danger to the animal's health and happiness and to avoid disappointment for you. This section will help you to prepare for your hedgehog's arrival.

Housing
Finding a proper cage is extremely important. Your hedgehog's cage will be its home and the place where it needs to feel safe and secure. There are a few bare minimum requirements for a hedgehog cage, as follows:
- solid flooring: Hedgehogs do not have feet that are equipped for wire flooring. They require a floor that is solid to avoid potential injury.
- space: Hedgehogs require a bare minimum of about 2-1/2 square feet of floor space. More is better when it comes to providing space. To calculate the square footage of a cage, measure the length and width in inches. Multiply the length times the width, then divide by 144. For example, a 25" x 18" cage would be 450 square inches, or 3.125 square feet. You also need to make sure that the cage layout is sufficient to fit all of the cage furnishing and accessories that you plan to include.
- ventilation: The cage must provide adequate ventilation without being too drafty. If moisture collects inside the cage, it is not sufficiently ventilated. If hedgehog becomes chilled frequently, this may be a sign that it is too drafty.
- security: hedgehogs are masters of escape. The cage should be secure enough that the hedgehog can not escape by squeezing out or scaling walls.

There are a wide variety of acceptable cage options that meet these criteria, but each has its pros and cons. This section will describe some of the most common cage solutions, as well as weighing their advantages and disadvantages.

Glass aquariums: A minimum size of 20 gallon long provides sufficient space. Aquariums can be easily escaped if there is no lid and a water bottle is hung from the side, so a wire lid that allows good ventilation and blocks escape is best. The biggest problem with aquariums is that they are very heavy and bulky when cleaning. They are readily available at pet stores, but can be quite pricey.

2a. There are a variety of wire guinea pig cages, such as this one, that are suitable for hedgehogs. Make sure that all cage surfaces are solid.

Wire cages: Only wire cages with solid bottoms, such as those made for guinea pigs, are acceptable. There are a wide variety of these available and they are easy to find in pet stores and pet catalogs. Some of the plastic-bottomed guinea pig cages are quite nice, though hedgehogs can scale the wire and can escape if they are not securely latched. Hedgehogs can fall when they climb cage sides, so a hedgehog that is prone to climb may not be a good candidate for a wire cage. They can also develop an abscess on the nose from trying to squeeze through wire holes that are only big enough to admit the nose. If you are raising babies, you will need to make sure that there is a "baby guard" or that the wire is no larger than about ½" x 1" or they can escape. Wire cages are typically lightweight and easy to clean, with the added advantage that they are well ventilated and allow in plenty of light. However, this also makes it important not to place them in a drafty area.

Hand built wooden cages: The bonus to these is that the imagination is the limit, if you are building your own. The thing to remember is to finish all wood surfaces with waterproofing, and allow the waterproofing adequate time to dry in a ventilated area before putting your hedgehog in the cage. Water proofing is extremely important because urine can soak into the wood if it is unprotected, creating a permanent odor and creating risk of bacterial growth. Linoleum flooring can be installed for ease of cleaning. Bulkiness and difficulty to maneuver when cleaning can be a problem.

Kennel Cabs: Early books cite kennel cabs as the recommended housing of choice, because it was believed that hedgehogs needed darkness. Since then, it's been found that hedgehogs need a regular light cycle of 12 ro 14 hours per day, and the darkness of kennel cabs isn't necessarily conducive to this. Kennel cabs that are large enough to be a sufficient hedgehog cage are generally large enough to house a wheel, and they do have the advantage that they are easy to clean and readily available.

Storage Tote Cages: Instructions for assembling these types of cages can be found in the Appendix of this book. These cages have a number of advantages, being inexpensive, lightweight, and easy to clean. They also stack or can be organized on shelves. The difficulty with them is getting adequate ventilation while still making them escape proof. Please see the section of this book on making things for your hedgehog for a photo and description of how to make these cages.

Wading pools: If you have the space, solid plastic wading pools with no ramp can make a spacious hedgehog habitat. The biggest disadvantage is that there is nowhere to attach a water bottle. While the size of the wading pool is bulky, it's easily cleaned by taking it outside and hosing it down. They are also fairly inexpensive and easy to find in spring and early summer.

2b. Storage tote cages are lightweight, easy to clean, and stack easily on shelving.

Environment

Once you have chosen your hedgehog's cage, it is important to think about the environment where you will keep it. The primary considerations are light, temperature, and noise. As previously mentioned, hedgehogs do need a light cycle. A room with a window that allows natural light works well, though you do not want to place the cage in direct sunlight. A dark closet is not a suitable place for a hedgehog cage, though hedgehogs kept under completely artificial lighting with a 12 to 14 hour daylight cycle do not appear to fare any differently than those who receive natural lighting.

Temperature is an extremely important consideration for hedgehog care. African hedgehogs are desert animals who come from a warm climate. They should be housed indoors, in a temperature-controlled environment and should never be left outside in a garage or other unheated area. Ideally, a temperature between 72 and 85 Fahrenheit is optimal. Hedgehogs appear to tolerate greater heat than greater cold. Long term exposure to cool temperatures can lead to hibernation attempts, which can be fatal, as well as decreased immune functioning, which is associated with increased chance of respiratory infections and susceptibility to mite outbreaks. While hedgehogs can tolerate very warm temperatures, they should never be left in a hot area that is unventilated or in direct sunlight.

Noise is also an important consideration and will depend somewhat on your hedgehog's temperament. If your hedgehog is outgoing and people-oriented, it will probably enjoy being located in a busy area of the home where it will receive a lot of notice and interaction. If your hedgehog is a scaredy cat, it will benefit from a cage location that is quiet and out of the line of traffic. Care should be taken to place hedgehog's cage where it will not be in danger of undue harassment by other household pets. Please see the section on hedgehogs and other pets for more considerations in this regard.

Feeding

In recent years, a number of companies have developed and marketed hedgehog foods, which vary widely in terms of nutritional content. Research has shown that captive hedgehogs need approximately 70 to 100 calories per day (1 to 3 Tablespoons of food) and that they need about 22% protein, 5% fat, and 15% fiber (Graffam, 1998). A young, active hedgehog or a pregnant or lactating female would need more toward the higher range of calories, while an older hedgehog with a low activity level would need fewer. Hedgehogs who are fed a high quality diet will likely eat less than those who are fed a low quality diet, just like we might eat a greater volume of lettuce while trying to get full than it would take to get full on hamburgers.

While many will assert that only one diet or another is sufficient, there are a wide variety of ways to arrive at an optimal diet. Many owners feed their hedgehog a mainstay of dry cat, dog, or hedgehog food that is always available for the hedgehog to feed upon. When evaluating a food, it is important to look for a fat content that does not exceed about 12% and that the food contains a quality protein, with meat as the first ingredient. Filler, such as corn, should not be the first ingredient. Meat, preferably not meat byproduct as that denotes lower quality, should be the first ingredient. It also should not contain colorful dyes, as these can create loose and colorful stools.

A wet cat or dog food should not be the mainstay of a hedgehog's diet because it provides no abrasion to reduce tartar buildup and may be higher in fat and sodium than the hard pellets. It should also be noted that there are foods on the market that are sold as hedgehog foods, but were never intended to be fed as a complete diet. Please read the box carefully and if it contains a high proportion of grains and nuts, it is not nutritionally appropriate as a mainstay for an African hedgehog though it may be offered as a treat if there are no peanuts or raisins. Many hedgehog owners use a combination of feeds in a mix, to increase the chances of providing a wide variety of nutrients.

2c. A mix of high quality hard foods, some bugs, and meant& vegetable baby food can be part of a healthy hedgehog diet.

It is often believed that because hedgehogs are insectivores, they must have insects in their diet. Dr. Graffam's (1998) reported that wild, hedgehogs consume beetles as a large proportion of their diet, and in captive hedgehogs, chitin from beetles appeared to help hedgehogs to better digest fat and improved fecal quality. The captive hedgehogs studied also seemed to utilize plant fibers in a similar manner. Thus, there is some suggestion that other dietary fiber can serve a similar dietary function. Insects that are chosen as part of a hedgehog's diet should be commercially raised, so as to be pesticide free, and should provide chitin to the hedgehog's diet. The advent of freeze-dried bugs in the pet market has made it easy to provide insect supplements.

Treat foods should be selected on the same basis as primary foods. They should contain good quality protein and/or fiber, and should be low in fat. Given the small amount of food that hedgehogs require, treats should be kept to no more than ½ teaspoon per night. Popular treats include cooked chicken or turkey, rice, sweet potato, apple sauce, lowfat yogurt, potato, meat and vegetable baby food, beans, watermelon, banana, chopped grapes, tofu, and cooked carrot. Not all hedgehogs enjoy treats, and not all captive hedgehogs will even eat bugs! You should try offering a food periodically before determining that it has been entirely rejected.

Several safety issues should be noted with regard to feeding. Hedgehogs should never be fed raw meat or eggs, as this can lead to bacterial infections such as salmonella. Wet foods or produce should never be left in the cage for more than about 4 hours, for the same reason. Foods such as whole or half peanuts can become lodged in the roof of a hedgehog's mouth, requiring a trip to the veterinarian for removal, and therefore should not be used. Hedgehogs are not rodents and cannot gnaw shelled nuts and seeds, nor does popcorn appear suited to their type of chewing.

It should be noted that hedgehogs can and will gorge themselves on favored foods, so hedgehogs who are overweight should be given limited access to food. Typical animal food safety issues regarding toxicity should be followed, such as no chocolate, hot dogs, potato chips, or other heavily processed foods. Hedgehogs are also presumed to be lactose intolerant and should not be fed cow's milk in any forms that do not contain active cultures to aid digestion.

Some owners choose to free feed their hedgehogs, offering a full food dish daily, while others prefer to monitor and, once a typical amount is established, only give as much as they expect the hedgehog will eat in a night. If you choose to free feed, you should still check your hedgehog's food intake on a daily basis. Loss of appetite can be an early sign of health issues or dental problems, in addition to the fact that hedgehogs are notorious for spilling or soiling their feed.

Exercise

Exercise is very important for hedgehogs. There have been several reports of children's science experiments using modified pedometers attached to hedgehog wheels that reported hedgehogs running 5 or more miles per night, at speeds of up to ten miles per hour. This should illustrate why it is important that hedgehogs have as much cage space as possible.

For many hedgehogs, running laps in a sufficiently large cage appears to be satisfying. Hedgehogs who are not satisfied with this will exhibit excessive escape-seeking behaviors and may even rub their noses bloody on the side of the cage. Use of a wheel can prevent these problems. Wheels used for hedgehogs should be at least 10 inches in diameter and must have a solid running surface. Hedgehogs do tend to eliminate while on the run, so the wheel should be easy to clean and disinfect, and it should be cleaned frequently to keep it clear of debris.

Out-of-cage time is another way to help hedgehog get his or her exercise. Some owners will allow their hedgehogs to free range in one or more rooms of the home. Two important considerations for this are cleanliness and safety. As on the wheel, hedgehogs are prone to eliminate where they are and may soil on the carpet. Hedgehog droppings are usually relatively small and firm, and can be cleaned readily. While hedgehogs are not in much danger of chewing on wires, as are rodents, hedgehogs can squeeze into some amazingly tight spaces, and may not be able to squeeze themselves back out. Get down to hedgehog eye level and make sure there is nothing that would be unsafe to squeeze into or behind, no avenue for escape, and nothing toxic that can be ingested. Recliners, heater vents, plastic bags, and appliances are particular dangers that should be avoided. If you are concerned about your hedgehog's safety when out and about, a large critter crawler ball, now readily available at most pet stores, would be an excellent solution, as long as you do not let it near the stairs and do not let anyone knock it around as this can cause stress or injury to the hedgehog.

Bedding

There are a wide variety of commercial beddings available, as well as noncommercial options. There has been a lot of controversy in recent years about what makes appropriate bedding for hedgehogs. This author is of the opinion that, of the bedding options that are commercially available, cedar is the only one that is completely unacceptable for hedgehogs. While it smells lovely and is probably acceptable for large animals, it is not suitable for small animals who are unable to get away from the fumes and for whom the phenols, which cannot be baked out of the cedar, can be highly toxic (Johnston, 1999).

Pine can carry dangers similar to that of cedar, though curing (baking) the pine to remove the phenols appears to reduce or eliminate these types of problems. We personally have seen many instances of skin allergy in hedgehogs that were kept on cedar, which we have not seen on hedgehogs kept on cured pine bedding, nor do hedgehogs kept on cured pine appear to have any differences in causes of morbidity or reduced lifespan as compared to those kept on beddings that are not wood based. It should be noted that the pine sold in feed stores for use in horse pens and other large animal enclosures is typically not well cured and should not be used with small pets unless it is very obviously well dried and

2d. Baby blankets with finished edges, alfalfa pellets, and pine shavings are all possible options for hedgehog bedding.

is shavings, rather than sawdust or chunks. Aspen wood is generally accepted as safe for small animals, though it is more expensive than pine and occasional instances of individual hedgehogs with aspen allergy have been noted.

Corn cob litters can be used as hedgehog bedding. The disadvantages are that it molds easily, though treated versions are available, and it should not be used with males due to high incidence of cases where corn cob becomes lodged in their penile sheath.

Recycled newspaper pellets or puffs are a popular hedgehog cage bedding. The disadvantages are that they smell like wet newspaper in the event of a water bottle leak and may also be gray, giving a dingy look to the cage. Another potential disadvantage is that these beddings can be deadly if ingested, due to creating blockage or expanding in the throat, although incidences of this type are not common. Traditional newspaper can also be used with hedgehogs, although light colored hedgehogs may appear dirty as the ink rubs off.

Pelleted beddings such as pelleted pine, pelleted newspaper, or even rabbit food pellets, can make good hedgehog cage bedding. The disadvantage is that they are heavy and will crumble when wet. Some hedgehogs may evidence skin allergies to the rabbit food pellets. Fireplace pellets or horse barn pellets are sometimes used, and are sold bulk so as to be less expensive overall. Be certain that they have not been treated with any chemicals that would be harmful to your hedgehog before using.

Nonclumping cat litter can be used in litter boxes, but is generally too dusty to use in an entire cage. Clumping cat litter should never be used with small animals due to its tendency to stick to damp spots, obstructing urination and defecation. It also has the potential to create intestinal blockage if accidentally ingested. As a side note, some hedgehogs naturally use one portion of the cage to do their elimination, and a litter box placed in this area will result in natural use of this area. Other hedgehogs do not take to litter training at all.

2e. A typical water bottle and food dish.

Cloth beddings are also commonly used. The most important safety issue is making sure that there are no loose threads as these can wrap around limbs and cut off circulation. For this reason, terry cloth towels are not suitable. Probably the most popular cloth bedding choice is vellux, which is typically cut up from old blankets and can be sewn into a layered, absorbent pad. Cloth beddings will need to be changed out and cleaned frequently in order to maintain odor control and hygiene. Some hedgehogs may chew on the vellux, which can create intestinal blockage if enough is eaten. A particularly ingenious response to this problem is a cage liner, commonly known as the Arata liner in honor of its creator, that is made from layers of vellux that are seamed inside a corduroy lining.

As a final note on bedding, it is possible for individual hedgehogs to be allergic to any of the possible bedding options, so what may work well for one hedgehog may not for another.

Cage accessories and toys

There are several cage accessories that are absolutely necessary for hedgehogs. These include a place to hide, a source for clean water, and a food dish. There are many options available for suitable hedgehog hiding places. Cloth pouches with finished edges, called hedgebags, are often used for hiding places. Old T-shirts, small cardboard boxes, wooden boxes, large half-logs, flower pots, and plastic igloos are also commonly used. If using cloth with your hedgehog, it is extremely important to make sure that there are no loose threads because these can get wrapped around a limb, creating a tourniquet effect that can lead to loss of circulation and loss of limb. It should be noted that the half-logs are quite difficult to clean and sanitize, and will likely need to be disposed of if hedgehog contracts mites.

Hedgehogs are generally able to utilize a water bottle. A four to eight ounce bottle with a metal drinking tube, hung so that the end of the drinking tube is about shoulder height, works well for most hedgehogs. Some owners prefer to use a water dish because they believe that hedgehogs can break their teeth if they chew on a water bottle tube. Because of this habit, water bottles with glass tubes should never be used, but actual instances of hedgehogs injuring themselves with water bottles are extremely low. Water dishes used should be small, about three to four ounces, and will need to be cleaned frequently. Hedgehogs do have a tendency to soil or throw bedding into their water dishes. Small crock dishes or plates, such as those made for hamsters, make good hedgehog food dishes.

Many hedgehog owners consider a wheel a necessary item for hedgehog health. If the hedgehog has enough space to run, a wheel is not absolutely necessary, but is generally considered a good idea. A hedgehog wheel needs to have a solid running surface and must be at least 10" in diameter. There are a variety of wheel designs that are acceptable. Many hedgehogs eliminate while on the run, so you will want to select a model that will be easy for you to keep clean. It should be noted that some hedgehogs do exhibit obsessive wheeling behavior, to the point that it can be detrimental to the hedgehog's health. If the hedgehogs is wheeling to the extent that it does not eat, repeatedly runs until it falls asleep on the wheel then gets up and begins to run again, or wheels to the point that it vomits, you may need to limit your hedgehog's wheel time.

In addition to the necessary cage items, hedgehogs also enjoy environmental stimulation. Any kind of toy that can be pushed, climbed, or manipulated is fair game as a hedgehog toy. The toy should be checked to make sure that it has no sharp edges, hedgehog cannot get stuck in it, it has no loose threads, and it won't be lethal if ingested. Favorite hedgehog toys include toilet paper tubes, cat balls, plastic eggs with food or a bell inside, small boxes that can be climbed in or on, small cars, small stuffed toys, squeaky toys, and toy dump trucks large enough for the hedgehog to climb on.

I have had reports of people whose veterinarians told them that the hedgehog would need a large water bathing dish, but this is not appropriate for an African hedgehog. They are generally not particularly fond of bathing in water and would likely just spill it or soil it. Further, it could present a drowning danger to young hedgehogs.

2f. A toy car provides stimulation for the hedgehog. Make sure there are no sharp edges.

Check your attitude and expectations

It is extremely important to remember that, unlike dogs and cats, hedgehogs have not been domesticated very long and will exhibit a lot of "wild" behavior. Because of this, fearfulness of new things is not surprising. Even the friendliest of hedgehogs raise their quills, and if you own a hedgehog you will get poked. It is also important to remember that many hedgehog behaviors, such as reactivity to sudden noises, fast movement, or handling, may not improve with time spent socializing the hedgehog.

To really enjoy hedgehogs, we have to sometimes make adjustments in our expectations. We can't expect that hedgehogs will be naturally calm and seek out our company. Some may do that, but they are definitely in the minority and it cannot be expected. Some naturally friendly hedgehog babies become very cranky when they go through quilling. This can take about one to four months to get over with. Some hedgehogs are just naturally cautious and there are those few who are simply aggressive.

It is important to remember that even the scaredy cat or hermit hedgehogs have their strong points. It isn't that they don't like you, it's that you scare them. It takes time to earn their trust and to learn how they want to be interacted with. Some hedgehogs will never enjoy being picked up, but will happily come to you and walk on you. Other hedgehogs may snort, snuffle, and prickle before being picked up, but calm down once in your lap. Each hedgehog is unique, and in order to have a satisfying relationship with you hedgehog, you must be prepared to accept the hedgehog for what it is, rather than expecting it to conform to what you want. up. Each hedgehog is unique and different, and for those hedgehogs who don't easily meet our expectations, the challenge is up to us to try to find the ways to interact that are enjoyable for both human and hedgehog.

Finding a veterinarian

Although hedgehogs are gaining in popularity, it can still be difficult to find a veterinarian who is willing to work with them. Because health problems can arise and progress rapidly, it is very important that you do your homework ahead of time and have a veterinarian identified before you need to find veterinary care for your hedgehog. There are several ways to go about finding a veterinarian.

The first place to look for a veterinarian is by word of mouth. If you know other people who own hedgehogs in your area, ask them where their hedgehogs get veterinary care. If this fails, check the phone book for veterinarians who are willing to see exotic animals. Those who will see birds, ferrets, or guinea pigs will often have seen at least a hedgehog or two.

If these methods fail, the next suggestion would be to check with your closest university veterinary program. They may be able to refer you to a graduate in the area who can help, or act as a consultation resource for a local vet. You may also want to check with Internet mailing lists, even those who deal with other species of small exotics, to see if anyone in your area has suggestions.

Sometimes veterinarians who have not seen hedgehogs before, but who have a good fund of knowledge regarding other small animals and are willing to work with you are a good choice. The October 1999 issue of Veterinary Medicine magazine provides an excellent overview of hedgehog care, including blood values and medicine dosages, and descriptions of common ailments. In addition, the health section of this book will assist a veterinarian in applying their general animal knowledge to hedgehogs by providing an overview of common ailments and symptoms. You may want to present your veterinarian with both of these resources if they are not familiar with hedgehogs.

If you are not satisfied that you have found a suitable veterinarian, it may not be the most appropriate time to purchase a hedgehog. Hedgehogs can often hide it when they are not feeling well, so that by the time you see symptoms, they are really sick and need care immediately. Veterinarians typically report that the most frequent reasons they see hedgehogs are for mites and for upper respiratory infections. Both are fairly simple and inexpensive to treat if caught in the early stages. Unfortunately, many report that they don't see the animals until it is too late to do much for them. Don't be caught by surprise. It may take some effort to find a vet who can treat hedgehogs, but it's well worth every second!

Finding the right hedgehog for you

Now that you have done all of your groundwork to prepare for your hedgehog's arrival, it is important to turn your sights to choosing the hedgehog that will be right for you. You can expect that a hedgehog will live approximately 3 to 6 years, so you are making an investment in a household member who will be with you for a long period of time. Considering this, it is generally not a good idea to make an impulse purchase. If you have the luxury in looking at and handling more than one hedgehog, do so. Make a list for yourself of the things that you want in your hedgehog (general personality type, age, gender, color, health, and any of the other things we have discussed so far), then rank each in the order of importance to you. Note which would be necessary for you, and which would be secondary. Measure each hedgehog that you consider against your own priorities. If you purchase a hedgehog that does not possess the qualities that you consider necessary, then it will not be a good match for you or the hedgehog. It is much better to wait and find the hedgehog that feels like a good match, rather than choosing based on immediacy, cost, or convenience.

Chapter 3: When hedgehog comes home

Once you've gotten your hedgehog's new home ready, found a veterinarian, have food and other supplies on hand, and have found the hedgehog that is right for you, the next step is bringing hedgehog home! Transition from one environment to another is always a stressor, no matter how much care has been taken. The tips in this chapter will help you to make that transition easier, minimizing the degree of stress that you and your hedgehog experience as hedgehog becomes part of your family.

Handling hedgehogs

Q: "How do you handle a hedgehog?"
A: "Very carefully!"

As reflected in the joke above, many people are understandably intimidated when dealing with an animal that has quills over the top half of its body and has the ability to roll into a tight, prickly ball. The pictures and hints in this section will help you to become more comfortable and confident in handling your hedgehog, which will increase your hedgehogs confidence and comfort with you.

The first thing to remember is that hedgehogs feel secure when they have safe footing. Holding a hedgehog upside down in a ball is not harmful to the hedgehog, but does not encourage it to feel secure. In order to help the hedgehog feel most secure, it helps to hold your hands loosely to the hedgehog's side (Photo 3a). Keep your hands relaxed as you slide them under its belly (Photo 3b). This allows you to give the hedgehog firm footing and allows your hands to be more in contact with the soft belly fur than the sharp quills. Once the hedgehog realizes it has firm footing it will become relaxed in your hands (Photo 3c). If you re nervous when you handle your hedgehog, it may result in nervousness from the hedgehog, making it even more difficult to handle.

Some hedgehogs do not relax enough for you to be able to use this technique. If this is intimidating you to the point where you do not want to pick up your hedgehog, you may want to scoop up some of the bedding as you scoop up the hedgehog, to cushion your hand from the quills. Using gloves to handle your hedgehog should be a last resort, as they do not allow your hedgehog to adjust to your smell. It is better to handle a hedgehog with gloves than not at all, but remember that the smell of some gloves may bother the hedgehog, making gloves counterproductive. If this seems to be

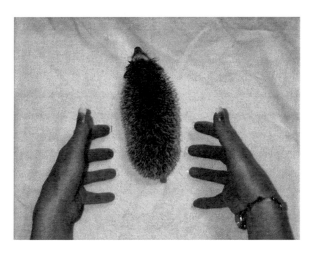

3a. To get ready to pick up a hedgehog, hold your hands loosely to the hedgehog's sides.

the case, try using a small blanket, T-shirt, or other soft cloth to cushion between you and the hedgehog. If you aren't getting prickled, you aren't as likely to get startled. If you are calmer and not easily startled, that will help your hedgehog to relax.

There is a hedgehog secret that helps balled-up hedgehogs relax. Hold the hedgehog in your hand if you are comfortable with that, or set it in your lap or any other comfortable setting, then rub its back in a gentle, circular motion. You can use your finger, fingernail, or even the rubber eraser end of a pencil to rub. It should be a firm, gentle motion (Photo 3d). Even a hedgehog who is completely balled up can be coaxed out by gently and patiently using this method.

Another tip for holding balled-up hedgehog is that distributing the weight of the hedgehog in your palm or palms decreases the amount of pressure that the quills exert on your hands. With years of practice, I can handle most hedgehogs without much discomfort. It is only the very heavy (more than 16 oz), very upset hedgehogs who can put enough pressure on their quills to actually break the skin. The quills are sharp, but not needle sharp. Yes, they can hurt, but the anticipation of how much we think it will hurt is often far more uncomfortable than the actual poke.

As a side note, if the idea of handling an animal that will prickle you at least occasionally sounds unbearable,

3b. Keep your hands relaxed as you slide them under the hedgehog's belly, in order to give the hedgehog firm footing.

then a hedgehog is probably not the best choice of pet for you. If it sounds like a something that you could get used to, then it just takes patience and practice. Different people definitely have their different levels of comfort, as do different hedgehogs. Don't worry about winning over your hedgehog on the first day. Patience and persistence are necessary qualities for forging a quality relationship.

Common adjustment difficulties

In addition to a higher level of defensiveness, common difficulties in the first few days can include nausea during the ride home, going off of food and water, green or loose feces, and excessive sleep or activity. Not all hedgehogs get carsick and those who get carsick generally don't get carsick every time. If your hedgehog gets carsick on the way home, make sure that any vomit on the hedgehog is cleaned off and when you get home, give your hedgehog access to clean bedding, fresh food and water, and if the hedgehog seems upset, give it some time to be alone and hide for a few hours before handling.

Higher levels of defensiveness in response to a change of environment, demonstrated by raised quills, huffling noises, and rolling into a ball, are not surprising, especially in young hedgehogs. Your home probably smells and sounds quite different than the hedgehog's previous home. It may have had a long journey by car or plane to

3c. This hedgehog is relaxed and calm.

get to you. Even a short journey in an automobile or a walk down the block may be very frightening changes. It is a good idea to keep the environment very calm for the first few days, and not to plan any outings, other than perhaps a well-pet visit with the veterinarian, for at least a week after your new hedgehog arrives. If your hedgehog is behaving defensively, yu may want to give it time to itself for the first two to three days before you start trying to handle your hedgehog. Talk to it in a quiet, calm voice to help it adjust to you. You can also provide a T-shirt that you have worn for your hedgehog to snuggle in, to help it adjust to your scent. These things alone won't necessarily lessen your hedgehog's defensiveness, but will help your hedgehog to experience your scent and voice as less threatening.

3d. This hedgehog is slowly relaxing in response to having his back rubbed in a firm but gentle circular motion.

Feeding issues are also quite common during the adjustment period. To help ease your hedgehogs transition, try to find out what food it was eating before you got it. Unless it was a completely inappropriate diet, obtain a sample of that food so that if you are unable to duplicate it, you can mix the old food with the new food to ease the transition. Start with about a 50/50 mix, then gradually increase the amount of the new food and decrease the amount of the old food in the mix until it is only the new food. Be sure to ask the person from whom you are getting the hedgehog if there are any foods that it definitely does not eat. Some hedgehogs can be very picky eaters and you don't want to spend a lot of money on something that it won't eat. Keep in mind that a young hedgehog's tastes may change and what it will eat today, it may not eat tomorrow. Foods that are refused should be tried periodically for the first few months before deciding they are completely rejected.

Sometimes people become worried because their hedgehog is not eating very much. Please keep in mind that an adult hedgehog typically only eats about one to three Tablespoons of food per night. If your hedgehog is not eating at all, try giving it a small amount of treat food, such as a little piece of cooked chicken, to see if it has any appetite. If it is eating small amounts of food and will accept the treat, then you probably have nothing to worry about. If your hedgehog is not drinking, you may want to consider that it doesn't like the taste of the new water. Getting a bottle of water from the person from whom you get your hedgehog and using that for the first few days, while gradually mixing in more of your local water, will help ease that transition. Another problem may be if you are trying to use a type of bottle or dish that the hedgehog is not accustomed to using. Try offering an alternate source of water or using bottled water to help determine the cause of the problem. Hedgehogs will generally only drink one to three ounces of water per night, so this level of consumption should be considered normal.

Green or loose feces are a common stress reaction in hedgehogs. While these things can be a sign of serious problems, they can also occur as a transitory signal of minor stressors. Planning a well-pet visit, to include a fecal float, as part of your hedgehog's introduction to its home will allow the veterinarian to help you make the determination of wether "the greenies" or "the runs" are a normal stress reaction or a problem to worry about. Under normal circumstances, stress related changes in fecal quality will typically clear up in about 3 days. If they do not, you may want to consider using a single food (ask the veterinarian for suggestions) and bottled water. This will typically help the problem to clear within a few days and new foods can be added, one at a time, when the problem clears. You will need to observe the effect of each new food on stool quality, to make sure the hedgehog tolerates the new foods.

Finally, excessive sleep or exercise are also common reactions to environmental changes. Hedgehogs are largely nocturnal and it should be expected that they will sleep a lot during the day. Baby hedgehogs will sleep a lot in general. What is important to notice is whether the hedgehog becomes alert and reactive when you pick it up. You should also check for signs that the hedgehog has been active when you aren't looking, such as food and water consumed, droppings in the cage, or rearranged cage furnishings. If it appears lethargic, then it may be sick or cold. If the hedgehog doesn't improve when warmed up, you will want to have a veterinarian check to make sure that it is healthy. If the hedgehog is overactive, you will want to make sure that it has a wheel or sufficient area in which to roam, to make

3e. This hedgehog is rolled into a ball. This is a typical defensive behavior, The hedgehog can not shoot its quills, but they are sharp.

3f. This hedgehog is partially raising his quills, as if to say, "I'm not sure I fully trust you."

sure that it doesn't engage in dangerous behaviors such as rubbing its nose on the side of the cage or climbing wire walls.

Understanding behavior/communication

Hedgehogs have several typical behaviors that they use to communicate how they are feeling. These include rolling into a ball, popping noises, raising quills, "huffling" noises, charging, purring, "whiffling" noises, licking, scratching, singing, peeping, screaming, and lethargy.

- Rolling into a ball: This behavior is clearly defensive. A hedgehog has amazing muscles that allow it to roll into a ball to protect itself. In the ball, it can maneuver its quills to face toward the direction from which it perceives the threat is coming. It can also perform a popping behavior, where it can pop up to half an inch in the air. This behavior allows it to discourage predators. If your hedgehog is rolled up in a ball, that probably means that it is feeling threatened and is trying to get you to leave it alone. Please note that while you can use the suggestions noted in the handling section to encourage your hedgehog to unball, you should never attempt to force it to unball as this could cause injury.
- Popping noises: These noises generally go along with being rolled into a ball and popping into the air. They have also been described as clicking. To make this noise, the hedgehog actually clucks its tongue against the roof of its mouth. This is a noise that is meant to intimidate and scare off something that the hedgehog considers threatening.
- Raising quills: Raised quills are another hedgehog defense. The hedgehog may be completely unballed but have its quills at "half mast" or may only have the forequills raised. This is to tell you that it is feeling somewhat threatened and uneasy with some aspect of the environment.
- Huffling noises: The word "huffle" has been coined to describe the huff and puff noises that hedgehogs make when they are upset. If your hedgehog is huffing and puffing (and maybe even snorting) it is trying to communicate that it isn't happy about something in the environment and is trying to make it go away.
- Charging: A charging hedgehog will usually have its forequills raised and will be making huffling noises. This behavior is typically a reaction to threat. You may see a hedgehog charge another hedgehog that it feels is infringing on its territory. A mother hedgehog with babies in the nest is likely to charge any hand that gets

to near, and a hedgehog who is very attached to his or her food dish may charge when you try to take it out.
- <u>Purring</u>: Hedgehogs have two different forms of purring that have been observed. The first is an aggressive purring that is often a precursor to the popping. The hedgehog will usually have its quills raised and will make a very loud purring noise to attempt to scare away a threat. There are also reports that some hedgehogs will emit a soft purr when they are relaxed and content.
- <u>Whiffling noises</u>: Whiffling, also thought of as whistling, is a term that has been used to describe a very soft sniffing noise that relaxed hedgehogs make when they are exploring. This noise is usually accompanied by quills down and nose in the air. It indicates that the hedgehog is relaxed and curious.
- <u>Licking</u>: Hedgehogs typically lick when they find something that smells tasty. If your hedgehog licks you, it is probably planning to try an exploratory nip if what it licks tastes as good as it smells.
- <u>Scratching</u>: Hedgehogs will often scratch because it feels good. It may not be communicating anything in particular. If your hedgehog is scratching excessively, it may mean that there is some skin irritation. Continued excessive scratching would mean that you should take the hedgehog to the veterinarian to make sure that there are no skin problems. Scratching would be considered excessive if the hedgehog is scratching to the point where it causes red spots or scrapes to the skin. Hedgehogs who are under 6 months old may seem to scratch a lot because they do have skin discomfort caused by emerging quills.
- <u>Singing</u>: Singing is typically a courtship behavior for hedgehogs. The male hedgehog will sing to the female as he attempts to convince her to mate. Singing can also be a dominance behavior and should be considered as a sign of possible aggression if a hedgehog is singing to another of the same gender.
- <u>Peeping</u>: Hedgehog babies will typically peep as a way to get their mother's attention. This behavior has occasionally been observed in adult females who cohabitate with other females and appears to be a way of communicating contentment.
- <u>Screaming</u>: Hedgehog screams are often referred to as "the hedgie scream of death." It is a very loud, piercing scream that is not soon forgotten. The scream is often a reaction to being hurt. There are also instances of hedgehogs who scream in their sleep or those who scream out of frustration. There is a legend about an owner who responded to a piercing hedgehog scream, only to find a hedgehog who loved to run in her wheel was standing back and screaming at another hedgehog who had lodged herself under their communal wheel, making it immobile. Despite the possibility of false alarms, a hedgehog scream should always be taken seriously and you should check the hedgehog thoroughly to make sure that there is no injury.
- <u>Lethargy</u>: This is not so much a behavior as a symptom, but is included in this section due to its importance for your hedgehog's health. A hedgehog who shows a sudden, drastic decrease in energy is telling you that he or she does not feel well. The most common cause of lethargy is hibernation, which is often accompanied by defensiveness and the hedgehog feeling cool to the touch. If the hedgehog cannot be returned to normal by warming or the hedgehog appears lethargic and limp, it is cause to seek veterinary advice immediately.

- <u>Pouting</u>: Hedgehogs can appear to pout if something in their environment seems out of place to them. This behavior is usually expressed as being grumpy, biting, huffling, resisting handling, and so on, in a hedgehog that does not ordinarily demonstrate these behaviors. The hedgehog may also exhibit reduced food intake and decreased activity levels. Hedgehogs can pout for a variety of reasons, including the owner being away, the cage being rearranged, or even having their wheel removed for cleaning. Pouting typically lasts for a day to a week. Care should be taken not to confuse pouting with medical issues, and if you are in doubt, always consult your veterinarian.

Behavioral issues

There are three major areas of behavior that I felt warrant their own specific sections due to the amount of concern they raise for new owners. These are biting, quilling, and self-anointing.

Biting

Hedgehogs are seldom overtly aggressive, but the maxim "anything with teeth may bite" certainly applies. In order to know how to manage biting behavior, you have to look at why the hedgehog is biting. The most common reason is because there is something on your hands that smells yummy and the hedgehog want a taste. In this case, the hedgehog will lick first and the bite is more of a nip. In this case, the hedgehog is not being mean or aggressive, it is just curious and exploring the environment. When a hedgehog nips, it is usually the surprise that is more uncomfortable than the actual nip. Keep in mind, hedgehogs can find some strange things yummy, like tobacco or soap smells, so this may be occurring even if you have just washed your hands or haven't recently had anything you'd consider yummy. Probably the best way to manage this kind of biting is what behaviorists call response prevention. Watch carefully, and if the hedgehog licks or shows any other sign of biting, move your flesh so the hedgehog simply cannot bite.

In young hedgehogs, nipping is definitely a way of exploring the environment. This may or may not be preceded by a lick. To discourage this behavior in babies we think have gone overboard with the exploratory nibbling, you can use a mildly aversive "air puff" technique. To do this, watch the hedgehog carefully and as soon as it begins to open its mouth, blow a puff of air toward its face. The hedgehog's natural response is to lower the visor or ball up. It can't bite when it's doing that and it usually only takes about 2 to 4 times of doing this for hedgehog to learn that trying to bite something that smells like you leads to something uncomfortable, and to stop.

In hedgehogs who don't usually bite, biting is probably a way for the hedgehog to communicate something. Your challenge is to figure out what. Some hedgehogs do not like to be handled for very long or may become uncomfortable in a noisy environment, and the bite is their way of saying, "This is too much. Put me down." Usually the hedgehog will squirm and otherwise let you know it's not happy with the situation before it bites, so learning to be attentive to what hedgehog does before the bite can help you to keep hedgehog happy so he or she doesn't have to bite to express displeasure. You should also remember that setting a hedgehog down and leaving it alone when it bites can teach the hedgehog to bite you in order to be left alone, so you will want to make sure that you don't allow this type of pattern to occur.

There are a small number of hedgehogs who bite consistently, for no apparent reason. It is important to rule out health concerns as a possible reason, as hedgehogs may bite because they don't feel well and don't want to be handled. There are a very few hedgehogs who just do not like to be handled, either because of fear or because they simply don't enjoy being handled. If your hedgehog bites consistently, the best thing to do is to practice handling techniques that keep you out of range of its teeth.

Quilling

Hedgehog quills are like human hair in that hedgehogs gain and lose them throughout their lifetime. Young hedgehogs go through several specific sets of quills before they get their adult set of quills and this creates a period of discomfort. The sets of quills that they get between the ages of about 6 weeks and 6 months appear to cause the greatest degree of discomfort, as evidenced by increased defensive behavior. The increased defensive or grumpy behavior of this phase, much like the discomfort related grumpiness of a teething human infant, is referred to as quilling. This behavior may include huffling, balling up, raising quills, popping, or even biting.

How can you tell if your hedgehog is quilling? Age is the first clue. Not all hedgehogs go through this phase, and some may only exhibit the increased grumpiness for a small portion of the time. If the hedgehog is between 6 weeks and 6 months of age and has a bout of grumpiness, it may be associated with a particularly uncomfortable bout of quilling. The second clue is lost quills. Most of the quills that you will see lost during this time period are small and thin, as compared to the quills that are growing in. The third clue that your hedgehog is quilling is that if you look at the skin, you can see new quills poking through in various stages of emerging. While your hedgehog is quilling, you do need to be aware that they can develop ingrown quills, much like ingrown hairs. Most of the time, these problems correct on their own. Occasionally, an ingrown quill will become infected and require veterinary care.

If your hedgehog is very defensive during the quilling stage, it is important to remember that if you allow the hedgehog's defensive behavior to scare you off, it will continue to act in this manner because it will not learn that you are friendly. Quiet lap time with gentle words and the offering of small quantities of treats is a great way to develop a rapport with your hedgehog, and to learn ways to interact that are comfortable for both of you. Some hedgehogs grow out of the quilling phase and become much calmer and more easily handled, often seemingly overnight, while other hedgehogs may never become entirely friendly.

Self-anointing

Self-anointing is a distinctly hedgehoggy behavior. When a hedgehog encounters a new smell in the environment, it often reacts by licking or chewing on the source of the smell, frothing up a lather in the mouth, then making the most amazing contortions to spread the lather on the forequills, back, and so on. No one is completely sure why hedgehogs do this. Some theorize that it allows them to blend their scent with the environment, thus helping to hide from predators. However, this doesn't necessarily make sense if you consider that it's usually unusual smells that they anoint with. Some

say that they do it to spread potential poisons on the quills, to make themselves more toxic to predators. Hedgehogs are purported to have an amazing resistance to many neurotoxins that makes this possible to do without injuring the hedgehog. A third theory suggests that new scents overload the scent receptors and they anoint to clear the neurons. Regardless of why they do it, it's an amazing feat to watch. Many persons are worried that their hedgehog has rabies when they see it frothing at the mouth, but they don't need to worry. Self-anointing is perfectly normal hedgehog behavior.

3g. This baby hedgehog is engaging in the behavior known as "self-anointing."

Hedgehog hide and seek ("hedgie-proofing")

Despite their funny little paws, hedgehogs are amazingly agile escape artists. The best time to prepare for hedgehog escapes is before they happen. You will need to make sure that the hedgehog cage is located in a secure room, so that you will know that your hedgehog has not gone far if it escapes. Hedgehogs can squeeze through very tight spaces, so the door should not have a large gap and outer doors of the home should always stay closed, unless you are absolutely certain that your hedgehog is secure.

If your hedgehog does escape, don't panic. Keep your cool and remember two thing. First, hedgehogs will come out at night, and second, there are some predictable patterns to where they are likely to hide. The first place to look is at warm and cozy spots in your house. Look near heater vents, behind the refrigerator, laundry piles or even in shoes. They also like dark spaces that seem safe- under recliners, under the sofa, under beds, and behind big things.

3h. Hedgehogs can quickly disappear under furniture, such as this recliner.

If you've searched the warm spots and the dark, cozy spots and you still can't find your hedgehog, it's important to make sure that the house is safe. Block access to any potential hazards, such as sump pump holes or plastic bags and be sure to check all laundry before washing if there's any chance the hedgehog might have access, as clothes make a very cozy hiding place. Next, put out a food and water dish in a place where you the hedgehog can easily find it. It is a good idea to put it near their cage, since hedgehogs are creatures of habit and will often return to familiar places. If there are any rooms you have checked thoroughly and are 100% sure the hedgehog is not hiding there, close them off so that you won't have to check them again. Most of all, make sure there is no way that hedgehog can gain access to the outdoors. If you can stay up very late at night to wait, the chances are strong that you will find your hedgehog waddling around and wondering why you seem so excited.

A live trap, such as the kind used to catch squirrels, can also be used to capture an escaped hedgehog. These traps can be obtained from many hardware or feed stores. If the outside of the wire is covered with a towel or blanket, it makes a dark hiding spot. To make it more tempting, you can put the hedgehog's food and water dish inside. Be sure to check at least morning and night for your escapee.

3i. If your hedgehog gets loose, be sure to check all of the dark, cozy spots where your hedgehog could hide. This hedgehog is making herself comfortable under a hassock.

Chapter 4: Keeping your hedgehog healthy

When to take your hedgehog to the vet

Providing appropriate health care is an important aspect of pet ownership. Veterinary care can be expensive and many hedgehog owners are understandably reluctant to take their hedgehog to the veterinarian for fear of running up high bills when there really isn't a problem. Please keep in mind that hedgehogs often don't show signs of illness until they are quite sick, so fast action can often mean the difference between life and death. When in doubt, you should always consult a veterinarian. The list of situations that follows is not meant as a substitute for veterinary care or consultation. It is meant to give you an idea of common situations that people frequently encounter, and to assist you in getting proper veterinary care. This list is meant to share with veterinarians who may not be familiar with hedgehogs and can also give you an idea of when you might want to request a second opinion. When deciding whether to seek veterinary care, it is always better to err on the side of caution and wen in doubt, call and let the veterinarian determine the urgency. If you and the veterinarian disagree about the urgency of the problem, remember that it is better to seek consultation that turns out to be nothing than to ignore something that turns out to be a big problem. All of these issues are potentially serious, but it should be noted that several items are clearly marked emergency because they are situations where immediate veterinary consultation or care is needed and even a brief delay may further endanger the hedgehog's health.

1. <u>My hedgehog collapsed and is limp</u>: EmergencyThis, obviously, is never a good sign. Get the hedgehog to the veterinarian immediately. Make sure to keep him or her comfortable and sufficiently warm, but not overheated.

2. <u>My hedgehog is having seizures</u>: Emergency
Call the veterinarian right away. You may want to have the veterinarian check the blood glucose level to rule in our out diabetes or hypoglycemia.

3. <u>My hedgehog is walking stiffly, falling over, or wobbling</u>:

This could be due to a wide variety of things- arthritis, injury, Wobbly Hedgehog Syndrome, etc... Call your veterinarian for a consultation and have him or her read the section of this book that covers wobbliness.

4. <u>My hedgehog has ingested household cleaner or other potentially toxic items</u>:
Call the veterinarian immediately. Some substances that are potentially toxic can be counteracted if treated right away, but are fatal if you wait. Better safe than sorry.

5. <u>My hedgehog appears to have a broken limb</u>: Emergency
Take the hedgehog to the veterinarian right away. A broken limb that is not set may heal incorrectly, causing discomfort later.

6. <u>My hedgehog has a runny nose and/or discharge from the eyes</u>: Emergency
Your hedgehog may have an upper respiratory infection. These are quite easily treated by a veterinarian, but may prove fatal if untreated.

7. <u>My hedgehog is acting funny</u>:
Behavioral changes are often an important clue. If an ordinarily friendly hedgehog suddenly becomes defensive and hostile, or a hedgehog who is ordinarily quite huffy suddenly becomes passive, this can be a sign to me that something is wrong. Visually inspect the hedgehog for sources of potential discomfort and make sure that the hedgehog is not chilled. A chilled hedgehog will be cool to the touch. It may ball up or raise its quills in a halfhearted way, or may simply seem very passive. If you cannot find a cause, consult the veterinarian within 24 hours.

8. <u>My hedgehog hasn't eaten for 24 hours</u>:
This isn't necessarily a problem. Sometimes hedgehogs go on a hunger strike for as much as a day to three, then resume their business normally. Female hedgehogs who are near to birthing may go off their feed for a day or so before delivery. If it persists longer than that or if there is notable weight loss, then you will want to schedule a vet visit right away. You will also want to check the mouth to make sure that there are no dental problems that are causing discomfort. Sometimes pieces of food can get lodged in the roof of the mouth or the hedgehog may have a tumor, an abscess, or a broken tooth. If the hedgehog has not consumed water for 24 hours, check to make sure that the water bottle is functioning properly. If you see any abnormalities in addition to the lack of appetite, call the veterinarian for a consultation immediately.

9. <u>My hedgehog is breathing, but is unresponsive and cool to the touch</u>:
The first thing I do is try to warm up the hedgehog, either by placing it under my shirt or placing it on a heating pad set on low, with a blanket between it and the hedgehog. The hedgehog may be trying to hibernate. If this doesn't help within an hour, then it may not be hibernation and should be considered an immediate emergency.

10. <u>My hedgehog has dry, flaky skin and/or is losing a lot of quills</u>:
If your hedgehog is young, the skin looks fine, and the quills lost are thin and small compared to the rest of the quills, the hedgehog is probably experiencing a normal

condition called quilling. However, if your hedgehog is older than about four months of age and the quill loss is excessive, causes bald patches, and/or is accompanied by dry and flaking skin, your hedgehog may have mites, a fungal infection, nutritional deficiencies, or just plain dry skin. A veterinarian can diagnose the cause and treat most sources of dry skin fairly inexpensively. Home remedies for mites are not generally effective and can wind up being more expensive, so you will want to see a veterinarian within 24 hours to make sure you are treating the correct problem in an effective manner.

11. <u>My hedgehog has ruffled ears</u>:
This can be caused by dryness or fungal infection. You can try putting a little cocoa butter on the ears at least once a day for several days. If it doesn't clear up, you will want to have a veterinarian check to rule out fungal infection rather than just dryness.

12. <u>My hedgehog has an ingrown quill that looks infected</u>:
When an ingrown quill gets infected, it may need to be lanced and cleaned by a veterinarian. It may also require antibiotics. Swift treatment helps to minimize discomfort and spread of infection, so you will want to see the veterinarian within 24 hours.

13. <u>My hedgehog has an unusual lump or bump</u>:
A number of studies have concluded that hedgehogs are prone to cancer. They can also develop cysts or abscesses that look like they might be tumors. The sooner a veterinarian can see the hedgehog and diagnose and treat the problem, the sooner the problem can be resolved so you will want to schedule a veterinary visit within the next 24 to 48 hours.

14. <u>My hedgehog has green stools</u>:
If it is tarry in consistency, get to the vet right immediately as this can often be a sign of organ problems. If the stool is loose, think about what the hedgehog has eaten in the last 24 hours. If it has had some new food or change of environment, it may just be mild gastrointestinal distress. If it persists for more than three days or appears gelatinous, you will definitely want to have fecal exam performed. Green stool is a general symptom of a very wide variety of things, some quite benign and some very serious.

15. <u>There are worms in my hedgehog's stools</u>:
Hedgehogs can get a variety of internal parasites, including tapeworms and round worms. These are not necessarily a sign of poor husbandry as they can be picked up from other animals, from contaminated insects that the hedgehog has eaten, or can be picked up if you let your hedgehog run around on the ground outside during supervised playtime. For this reason, you should never allow your hedgehog to eat wild caught insects. Internal parasites create a very serious health risk if left untreated and you should not attempt to treat with over the counter remedies. Sometimes a hedgehog can carry a parasite load and appears completely healthy until eventually the parasite load becomes sufficient that the worms are obvious in the stools. Seek veterinary care within 48 hours if you have any reason to suspect that your hedgehog has worms as the veterinarian can treat them effectively and inexpensively.

16. <u>My hedgehog has blood bubbling from its nose</u>: Emergency
As terrifying as this might be, this condition may not be fatal if you seek veterinary care immediately. Possible reasons can include injury, liver problems, or a heavy parasite load that is creating a strain on its system and inhibits blood clotting. Immediate diagnosis and treatment may make the difference between life and death.

17. <u>My hedgehog's eye(s) look cloudy</u>:
There can be multiple reasons for this symptom. Some infections may create this appearance, and must be treated with antibiotics. Cataracts can also give this effect. A veterinary consultation will be needed to make an appropriate diagnosis and determine whether your hedgehog needs treatment or simply monitoring.

18. <u>My male hedgehog's organ is swollen larger than the diameter of a nickel</u>:
Male hedgehogs, especially adolescents, can get things like bits of bedding stuck in their penile sheath, causing considerable discomfort and infection. The immediate thing to do if you see that the male has abnormal swelling in his genital area is to put lukewarm water in the sink to about his arm pit level. Allow him to wade around for a few minutes to clean the area, then see if there is any obvious debris that you can gently remove. Next, get him to the veterinarian for a double check, to make sure that there are no irritants remaining, and inquire as to the advisability of an antibiotic.

19. <u>My hedgehog has discharge from its ears</u>:
There are a variety of possible causes for this (see the section in this book on ear discharge) and it is very important that you seek veterinary care within 48 hours to obtain appropriate diagnosis and treatment.

20. <u>My hedgehog is urinating blood or green urine</u>: Emergency
Either of these conditions need immediate veterinary care. They may signify tumors or infections and must be attended to quickly in order to have a better chance that the ailment can be effectively treated.

21. <u>My hedgehog is crawling with bugs</u>:
In order to determine what you need to do, you need to be able to figure out what kind of bugs are crawling on your hedgehog. Some mites that can attack hedgehogs appear as very tiny insects in white, black, or red.
 are black, have a somewhat oblong appearance, and move very quickly. Mites typically require veterinary treatment, while fleas can often be treated at home (see the veterinary care section). If you are uncertain, ask your veterinarian for guidance. If the hedgehog shows behavioral abnormalities or any other symptoms of ill health besides the bugs, then this should be considered an emergency.

Common medical problems
Mites

Mites are probably the most frequently encountered medical issue with hedgehogs. There are a lot of myths and misconceptions about hedgehogs and mites, and this section addresses the three biggest ones. First, there is the idea that the mites that hedgehogs get are species-specific. That is not true. Several species of mites have been identified on hedgehogs, including those that can also affect dogs, cats, rabbits, livestock, and birds. Cases reported by members on an Internet mailing list include those identified by veterinarians as sarcoptes, psoroptes, chorioptes, and demodex.

The second mite myth is that mites are always a sign of poor husbandry. Certainly, poor husbandry isn't going to help the situation, but even if you are scrupulous about cleaning, you can have have mites turn up on your hedgehog. There are plenty of possible explanations that have been suggested. One is that mites can lay dormant in bedding. If you purchase a bag of infested shavings, you bring the mites home to your hedgehog. Second, mites can be present at an undetectable level. If you handle another animal outside the home, the mites get on you, and you bring them home to hedgehog. Or, your hedgehog may have just a few mites that are undetectable until something happens to create stress, like a chill or minor illness, and the mites take advantage of the weakened condition to multiply. Either way, you can be cleaning and disinfecting daily and still have a mite outbreak.

The third group of misconceptions has to do with treatment. The current standard of treatment from the veterinarian is three doses of Ivermectin injection, given two weeks apart. Amitraz has also been used as a dip, with the same three dose schedule. I have used Sealmectin for mite management since April of 2000 and have found this to be far more effective than either the Ivermectin or Amitraz. Research is currently underway to demonstrate the effectiveness of Sealmectin in hedgehog mite treatment and you should ask your veterinarian about this option. Home methods of treatment have been demonstrated to effectively treat hedgehog mites so a veterinary visit is always indicated if mites are suspected.

Symptoms of mite infestation can include dry skin, flaky or scabby skin, discharge around the ears, eyes and nose, quill loss, and sometimes visible mites. A skin scraping is used to differentiate dry skin that is due to mites from other possible causes. Quill loss with mite infestation can result in large patches of baldness, and in extreme cases, complete baldness. The quill coat typically grows back in after successful treatment. Quills that are lost due to normal shedding will often have a round bulb at the base, while those lost due to mite infestation may appear ragged and have skin attached.

As a final note on mites, sometimes mite eggs will be found in the fecal exams of hedgehogs who are experiencing a mite infestation. Apparently these mite eggs look quite similar to the eggs of liver flukes and there have been questions of differential diagnosis. If your hedgehog is diagnosed with liver flukes on the basis of eggs in a stool sample, you may wish to ask for a consultation with a second opinion. Most liver flukes require a snail as a vector for transmission so it is an improbable, though possible, diagnosis and the treatment protocols are not the same.

Respiratory infections

Respiratory infections are probably the second most common acute illness seen in hedgehogs. Symptoms include sneezing, a runny nose, or bubbles from the nose. The hedgehog may also be lethargic and cool to the touch in an advanced case. Hedgehogs are susceptible to bronchial pneumonias due to a variety of causes, such as

Bordatella, mycoplasma, bacterial infections, and environmental stress. If you suspect a respiratory infection, you will need to seek treatment immediately.

Tumors and abscesses

Every article I have ever read on hedgehog morbidity indicates that cancers are extremely common among hedgehogs, particularly those over 3 years old (Hoefer). All parts of the body can be affected: skin, mouth, nose, reproductive organs, liver, spleen, and so on. Symptoms of cancer can include lumps and bumps, blood in the urine, and weeping sores on the skin. Other signs that may be associated with cancer include weight loss, lack of energy, low appetite, and susceptibility to hibernation. Early detection increases the chance of effective treatment, so it is important to seek veterinary care as soon as possible.

Hedgehogs can also develop abscesses that need to be lanced and drained. If you suspect an abscess, you need to have a veterinarian care for it to ensure proper sterilization and to prescribe antibiotics to reduce the chance of further infection. An untreated abscess can lead to systemic infection and death.

Fatty liver

Fatty liver is a frequent necropsy finding in African hedgehogs. Because pet hedgehogs are often fed a diet that is high in fat and may not have ample room to exercise, they exhibit a high rate of obesity. High fat foods can strain the liver, as can extreme efforts to help the hedgehog lose weight. Making sure that your hedgehog's diet is not overly high in fat and includes sources of dietary fiber, as well as making sure that your hedgehog does not become obese, will help decrease the risk of fatty liver.

Fatty liver has also been associated with hedgehogs that have been off their feed, due to other medical problems. Force feeding foods that are too much for the system to process can create secondary problems with the liver so you should consult with your veterinarian as to appropriate feeding solutions for hedgehogs with compromised health.

Sometimes outwardly healthy hedgehogs have developed fatty liver problems. Symptoms include lethargy, lack of interest in food, and weight loss. Exploratory treatment with homeopathic methods have indicated that milk thistle has had some successes in reversing the progress of the fatty liver process. You should consult your veterinarian before attempting any treatment for such a serious condition at home and homeopathic practitioners have cautioned that milk thistle should not be given to healthy animals as a prophylactic measure due to potential side effects.

Dental issues

It has long been noted that dental problems are common in hedgehogs. Even hedgehogs as young as a year or two may exhibit tooth loss to the extent that it impairs their ability to eat hard foods. In the mid 1990s, it was fashionable for veterinarians to prescribe small toothbrushes and chicken flavored toothpaste to hedgehog owners, with the recommendation to brush daily. I suspect that these veterinarians had never attempted this task themselves. More practical things that people have done to assist their hedgehogs' dental health are providing crunchy foods for tartar control, checking the mouth periodically and having teeth scraped or removed if needed, and use of dental wipes or water additives that are now available at pet stores to help pet dental health.

Obesity

As previously noted, obesity is a common difficulty in pet hedgehogs. Because hedgehogs vary in the size of their body frame, there is not a particular weight that differentiates an obese hedgehog from one that is a healthy weight. Rather, you must look at the hedgehog to determine suitability of its weight. A hedgehog should be able to roll into a tight ball with no belly showing. If the hedgehog is too fat to close entirely into a ball, it is probably overweight. The hedgehog should also feel firm to the touch, not squishy, and should not have fat pockets in the arm pit areas.

If your hedgehog appears overweight, it is very important that you encourage it to get more exercise. You may wish to limit food amounts to one or two discrete feeding times

4a. This hedgehog has difficulty rolling into a ball and should be considered overweight.

during the day, removing the food when the feeding time is done. If the hedgehog still gorges, you may wish to feed a limited amount of food, such as 1 to 3 tablespoons. You may wish to scatter the food over the cage area to encourage natural foraging behaviors, as well as switching to a lower fat food. If your hedgehog does not respond to basic weight control measures, please consult your veterinarian to help you design a weight control program.

Ear problems

Hedgehogs can develop a variety of ear problems, including ruffled tips, crustiness, and drainage. While ruffled tips are usually not dangerous and typically reflect dryness or fungal infection, crustiness and drainage may signify bigger problems. If you notice drainage coming from the ear, the first thing that you will need to check is the consistency. If it is granular, it is most likely to be mites. This may seem shocking, as the ear may be clear one day and filled the next, but mites can cause that. If you have any suspicion that mites may be involved, it's usually best to go to the veterinarian right away to check for mites and to treat if they are found.

Yeast infections can also occur in the ear, typically evidenced by a discharge that appears gooey and is generally yellowish to brown. The discharge may also smell funny. To help with the immediate surface problem while waiting to get to the veterinarian, you may want to treat with a few drops of diluted peroxide (50% hydrogen peroxide, 50% water) or white vinegar solution (10% white vinegar, 90% water) solution in the ear. It is important to have a thorough veterinary examination to determine the source of the infection. There have been instances where this type of infection was associated with polyps in the ear or diabetes.

Wobbliness

Quite a bit of attention has been given to Wobbly Hedgehog Syndrome (WHS) in recent years. While a wobbly appearance can signify a wide range of problems, actual WHS is a chronic, progressive paralysis that typically starts with the hindquarters and progresses until the hedgehog is completely incapacitated. It has been observed to occur in hedgehogs of all ages and is believed to have an inherited component. At present, WHS can only be definitively diagnosed at necropsy.

With all the information that is available about WHS on the Internet, many people jump immediately to the conclusion that their hedgehog must be afflicted with WHS if it shows difficulty with gait, particularly if this is progressive. There are other conditions that can mimic the symptoms of WHS, so it is important to consult with a veterinarian immediately, in order to avoid losing precious time for treatable disorders.

The biggest thing that distinguishes WHS from other disorder is family history. There are at least two families that I am aware of that had confirmed cases in nearly all the members of two generations. If you don't know the lineage of your hedgehog, you won't have any information to help you with this part of the diagnosis. If you do your homework before you purchase your hedgehog and work with a breeder who is open with their records, and whom you trust to be accurate, you will know what is in your hedgehog's history. If you do suspect WHS, let the breeder know immediately and let them know the veterinary findings. This is very important in helping them to decide what lines to continue, and which should be retired if patterns of problems are found.

Hibernation is probably the most frequent cause of wobbliness in hedgehogs. There may be mild wobbliness or there may be significant lethargy. Hibernation is not safe for hedgehogs of African origins and they should not be allowed to hibernate. A hedgehog that is trying to hibernate is often cool to the touch. Onset is often rapid, although symptoms of mild wobbliness and lack of appetite can drag on for quite some time if the problem is not identified. Hibernation can generally be reversed within half an hour to an hour by warming up the hedgehog. Holding it under your shirt or providing a heat pad on low is generally sufficient. Do not use heat rocks as they often have hot spots that can cause burns and do not raise the ambient temperature.

Injury is another frequent cause of wobbliness. Hedgehogs can break legs or even slip disks. X-ray or ultrasound can be used to quickly determine whether an internal injury appears to contribute to the hedgehog's gait difficulty. Hedgehogs can also develop problems with excessive bone calcification, leading to progressive wobbliness. This can also be diagnosed with ultrasound or x-ray. External injury, such as overgrown nails that have curved into the pad of the foot or hairs wrapped around a leg can also cause a hedgehog to look wobbly, so you should visually inspect for these types of problems.

Tumors can also create problems with balance and locomotion. These can very strongly mimic WHS. Tumors of the abdomen or brain can create progressive difficulty with movement. These types of problems can sometimes be diagnosed by ultrasound or exploratory surgery and can sometimes be treated successfully by early detection and removal of the tumor.

Bacterial and fungal problems of the skin have also been reported to cause a wobbly appearance in afflicted hedgehogs. Hedgehogs with these types of problems are reported to have a noxious odor, in addition to seeming wobbly. At least one case of a hedgehog with allergic dermatitis that gave the appearance of wobbliness has been reported.

Strokes do occur in hedgehogs and can give the appearance of WHS. However, onset is typically fairly rapid. Early treatment can help to reverse some of the damage in many cases, or there may be slow, spontaneous recovery over time.   In rare cases, strokes have been identified in hedgehogs as young as nine weeks old.

Nutritional deficiencies can also create a symptom picture that looks like WHS. If you are concerned about dietary issues, consult a knowledgeable veterinarian about how your hedgehog's diet can be improved. If diet is the issue, you will see improvement with a healthier diet.

Definitive diagnosis of WHS is at present only possible with a necropsy. As you can see, there are many other things that can contribute to a similar symptom picture, so it should not be assumed that all wobbly hedgehogs have WHS, even if it "looks just like WHS." Please consult a veterinarian if your hedgehog exhibits wobbly behavior that does not reverse when it is warmed up and do not accept a diagnosis of WHS that is made in the absence of a family history and thoroughly ruling out other possible causes. While I have not talked personally with any veterinarians who are researching WHS, it is my understanding that at the present time, WHS is believed to be a Multiple-Sclerosis like disease that results in progressive demyelinization in the central nervous system.

Fleas

Just like dogs and cats, hedgehogs can get fleas. Fleas are very fast little black bugs and they leave tell-tale "flea trash," which looks like dark brownish crusty stuff, but is actually blood, on the quills. The best treatment is generally a puppy and kitten safe flea shampoo. Be sure to follow the directions, which typically include some time for the animal to set with the shampoo on it before rinsing. While the hedgehog sets with the shampoo, thoroughly clean the cage and treat the area around the cage with a dog and cat safe flea treatment. Most of these include pyrethrins as an active ingredient.

As an important caution, please carefully check any products before you use them on a hedgehog to make sure that they do not contain alcohol. Apparently alcohol is often used as a base for chemical products because it evaporates, leaving the chemical on the skin. Some of the alcohol is absorbed into the animal, and this can be very dangerous for small animals, such as hedgehogs. There have been several reported cases of toxicity from this, and it can be fatal. Most products that are labeled as safe for puppies and kittens are also safe for hedgehogs.

Cleanliness and bathing

1b. This hedgehog is bathing in lukewarm, ankle-high water in the sink.

Hedgehogs are not generally smelly animals and do not require baths on a regular basis. They do, however, have some cleanliness requirements. First, they have a tendency to do a lot of walking at night and this sometimes takes them back through their droppings, leading to feet that are caked in feces. To remedy this situation, you can put about half an inch (1 centimeter) of lukewarm water in the sink and allow your hedgehog to wade around in it for a few minutes. This helps to soften the feces so that you can scrub it off with an old toothbrush.

Healthy toenails are also a hedgehog cleanliness issue. Hedgehog toenails can sometimes become overgrown, curling into the feet and making it painful for the hedgehog to walk. You will want to check your hedgehog's feet weekly to ensure proper nail health. The nails are typically easier to trim when wet and soft. You can use a small pair of nail clippers to gently clip the nail to just above the quick. The quick is the area of flesh underlying the nail. Just like with your own nails, you want to clip the part that is away from the skin, and not too close to the skin. As long as they are not curling under and creating a problem, they are short enough. Styptic powder or corn starch will quickly stop bleeding if you accidentally nick the skin. If your hedgehog is uncooperative, you may want to ask the veterinarian or an experienced hedgehog owner to teach you techniques that will allow you to trim your hedgehogs toenails.

Hedgehogs can also require a bath if they have self-anointed with something unpleasant. To bathe a hedgehog, you will want to fill the sink with lukewarm water to about belly level. Allow the hedgehog to walk around in the sink and gently pour some water over the hedgehog to get it wet. Lather some puppy and kitten safe pet shampoo in your hands, then soap up the hedgehog. An old toothbrush can be used to loosen debris. Be sure to keep your hedgehog warm and out of drafts while it is drying.

Some hedgehogs may enjoy dust baths. I discovered this by accident when I had spilled chinchilla dust on the floor. One of my hedgehogs was running around on the floor and he started doing something kind of funny when he found it. At first I thought he was having a seizure. He dipped one shoulder kind of down into it and shook. Then he did it on the other side. After a couple of times, he rolled on his side in a ball and did what I can only describe as an upside-down shimmy in the dust. I quickly realized he was dust bathing. For some hedgehogs, even new shavings or kitty litter (please use the nonclumping variety only) may elicit a dust bathing response.

Communicating with your veterinarian

Sometimes people feel awkward when trying to talk with their veterinarian about their hedgehog. At the same time, the veterinarian is very dependent upon your knowledge of what is normal for your individual hedgehog. "He's acting funny," does not tell your veterinarian very much about what is going on, so you will need to be able to describe the problem to your veterinarian in as much detail as possible.

Many owners find that it is helpful to keep a notebook or scrap book with details and observations about their hedgehog.

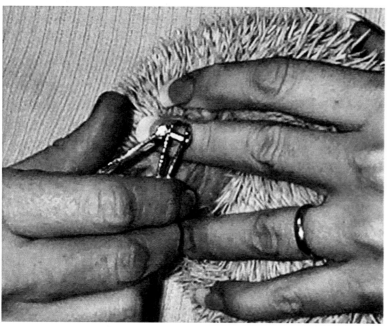

4c. This hedgehog is getting his toenails trimmed.

In this book, you will want to put details such as the hedgehog's birthday and any information about health issues in its lineage. You will also want to record observations such as weight, sleep patterns, eating patterns, favorite foods, any injuries that occur, and any instances of unusual behavior. Anything unusual in your hedgehogs environment should also be noted, such as introducing a new food or outings that the hedgehog has taken. Bringing this along to show your veterinarian will help him or her in understanding patterns of what is normal and what might be a sign of illness for your individual hedgehog.

What to keep in your hedgehog care/first aid kit

There are a number of things that are good to keep on hand for basic care and also in case of emergencies. Here are the items that I keep in my hedgehog care/first aid kit:
- Small nail clippers: Used to trim toenails
- Sterile saline solution: Used to clean and disinfect
- Old tooth brush: Used for cleaning quills and feet
- Puppy and kitten safe pet shampoo: Used for bathing
- Cornstarch: Used to stop bleeding quickly.
- Digital scale that weighs in grams: Used to measure the hedgehog's weight on a regular basis, since weight loss can be an early sign of medical issues.
- Hydrogen peroxide: Used for cleaning and disinfecting.
- Cotton swabs and cotton balls: Used for applying hydrogen peroxide or sterile saline.
- Cocoa butter: Used for treating ears that are ruffled due to dryness.
- Heat pad: Used to warm the hedgehog if it becomes chilled.
- Chicken baby food: Can be easily syringe fed if hedgehog is off its feed.
- 1 cc plastic syringe with pointy tip: Used to syringe feed if needed.

Chapter 5: Beyond the basics

Travel with hedgehogs

Every pet owner needs to prepare for the eventuality that they may need to travel. Hedgehogs should not be left alone for more than about 24 to 48 hours alone, especially if there are extreme weather conditions. Taking your hedgehog with you when you travel may be a possibility. Although most hedgehogs will exhibit minor stress reactions, they typically handle travel fairly well. Before making travel plans, be sure that it is legal to have hedgehogs where you are going.

If traveling by car, you will want to ensure that your hedgehog has a travel cage that provides space to stand up, sit down, stretch out, and walk around a bit. A cat-sized kennel cab makes a good travel cage. You will need to ensure that your hedgehog has suitable climate control. You do not want to expose your hedgehog to extreme cold or direct sunlight. You may want to bring a small pet carry pouch that you can use to place your hedgehog in if you need to stop for meals, rather than leaving the hedgehog in the car. It may not be practical to hang a water bottle in the travel cage while moving, so you will want to make sure to have a dish that you can use to offer hedgehog water when you make stops.

If traveling by airplane, you will need to make sure that the airline accepts hedgehogs on board. Most airlines that allow pets require that the hedgehog accompanies you in the cargo area, rather than in the cabin. It typically costs $50 to $100 each way for a pet to accompany. In order to travel, your hedgehog will need an airline approved kennel cab. A cat-sized kennel cab is appropriately sized. Use newspaper or any other absorbent bedding that isn't easily scattered to line the inside of the cage. The hedgehog will need to have a food and water dish attached, as well as a small bag of extra food taped to the top of the kennel. Inside the kennel, you should provide something for the hedgehog to hide in, such as a hedgebag, shredded newspaper, or blanket. You will need to use live animal labels as well as a shippers label on the outside. The airline can supply these if they do not come with the kennel cab. You will also need a veterinarian's health certificate that is no more than 10 days old at the time of travel. Do not try to smuggle your hedgehog on an airplane as this can result in being put off of your flight if it is discovered.

Hedgehogs and other pets

Many people wonder how their hedgehog will get along with other animals in their household, including other hedgehogs, other small animals, and their family cat or dog. Hedgehogs in the wild are pretty much solitary creatures who come together for mating, then go their separate ways. Babies stay with mother until weaned, then they, too go their separate way. While captive bred females may accept and even enjoy the company of other females, two males cannot be expected to tolerate one another. Even males who appear to get along at first can develop a territory dispute that becomes fatal to one or the other before the owner ever realizes what is going on. Because of this, it is absolutely not recommended to house two males together. A male and female should only be housed together for a brief period for breeding purposes because they will likely kill and eat the babies if they are together at the birthing. If you attempt to house two females together, supervise and be prepared to separate until you are certain that they get along. If you see signs of minor aggression, be sure to separate them. Hedgehogs may not look like they have much jaw power, but they can rip one another apart.

5a. These hedgehogs are in a kennel cab that is ready for travel.

Many people wonder if hedgehogs can be housed with other animals. This is just not a good idea. Being solitary, the presence of another animal, especially if it is active at times when the hedgehog is not, may create a considerable amount of stress. Different animals have different needs for feeding, for quiet, and so on. Feeds that are completely appropriate for rodents may contain seeds that are dangerous to hedgehogs because they can become lodged in the roof of their mouth. Stress can lead to illness in one or the other animal, as well as fighting. Hedgehogs should not be housed in the bottom of a bird cage. Even though the birds occupy the top level and the hedgehog occupies the bottom, wire bottomed cages are not safe for hedgehogs and living underneath animals that are voiding upon it just isn't sanitary. If you have another animal that is not a natural predator, such as a rabbit or guinea pig, you may be able to give both hedgehog and other animal room playtime at the same time. This should only be done under direct supervision and they should be separated if either animal appears disturbed.

Predatory animals, such as dogs, cats, and ferrets, may have very different reactions to hedgehogs. Some may ignore the hedgehog completely, while others may actively pursue it as potential prey. Hedgehogs do have the ability to intimidate most predators by rolling into a ball while loudly huffing and popping, but this does not dissuade all of them. Hedgehogs should never be left unsupervised in a place where a predatory animal has the opportunity to harass or harm them. Excessive barking from a

5b. This cat and baby hedgehog enjoy one another's company, but still should never be left alone together. Photo courtesy of Becca Loane.

5c. This dog's stance suggests that it views the hedgehog as a potential threat or prey. The dog may snap at the hedgehog.

dog or stalking from a cat or ferret can result in increased defensive behavior, such as refusing to come out of a ball, popping, and biting. If the other animal is not particularly interested in the hedgehog, it probably won't bother the hedgehog to be out at the same time, as long as you are there to protect, but don't leave it alone with a potential predator.

Hedgehogs in public settings

There are many public settings where hedgehogs are welcome, such as visiting pet stores or going to the park. Some just take hedgehog everywhere they possibly can. It is important to use common sense in deciding when and where to take your hedgehog out in public. First, it is important to consider whether your hedgehog's temperament is well suited to the public life. Snugglers are typically well suited to public outings, as they are typically calm and easygoing. Runners may not like to stay still, but may not be disturbed by the noise and changes of going out and about. Scaredy cats and hermits are not well suited to public outings and may find the experience quite stressful.

Places that are relatively quiet and pet friendly are good places to take your hedgehog. People may be very curious and ask lots of questions. If a place is very busy and active, please be sure that you can keep your hedgehog safe and secure while you are out visiting. There are many commercially available small pet carrying pouches that are quiet secure and offer a safe haven for a hedgehog on the town. Be sure that it is completely secure because it would be a tragedy to lose your hedgehog in a public area due to escape from its container.

If you decide to take your hedgehog outdoors, such as to the park, you should keep in mind that the outdoors presents many dangers for hedgehogs. They are busy, curious creatures and you can lose your hedgehog if you turn away for even a moment. Dirt harbors many parasites, as do wild insects, which your hedgehog can ingest, creating a health risk. You may not be able to control dogs or other harassing animals or people that come into the environment. There has even been a case of a hedgehog that was purportedly carried away by a hawk and other hedgehogs have been lost when they escaped while accompanying the family on a camping trip. Temperatures may be

5d. While a trip outdoors sounds like fun for your hedgehog, you need to be aware that the outdoors presents many dangers for your hedgehog.

too hot or too cold to be comfortable, creating stress for the hedgehog. Clearly, trips to the outdoors require considerable thought and planning, and in many cases are not advisable.

Hedgehog colors

Hedgehogs come in a wide variety of colors and patterns. The basic colors are formed out of a combination of shades of brown, black, and apricot. Common patterns include snowflake (20% to 80% of the quills have no bands), white (less than 5% of the quills have bands), and pintos (there are spots or patches of unbanded quills with pink skin underneath). To thoroughly discuss hedgehog colors is far beyond the scope of this book, and those interested in learning more about hedgehog colors should see Appendix A for additional resources.

When talking about hedgehog colors, one should understand what is meant by a color band and an unbanded quill. Think about the basic quill being solid white with no color. This is an unbanded quill. Then, look at the quills that have color. You will see that they tend to be white on the ends, with a colored area or areas in between. The colored part of the quill is what is referred to as a color band, and quills that have these color bands are referred to as banded quills.

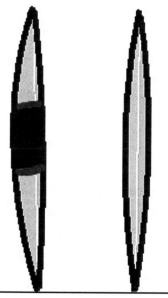

5e. These drawings represent a banded (left) and unbanded (right) hedgehog quill.

The International Hedgehog Association recognizes seven basic groupings of hedgehog colors: Standard, Apricot, Snowflake, White, Pinto, Albino, and Any Other Color. The Standard Class includes all dark colored hedgehogs whose quills all bear color bands and who have dark eyes. The Apricot Class includes the hedgehogs whose color bands are in the lighter end of the spectrum. Many of them will have red eyes. Snowflake hedgehogs may have color eyes and quill bands. What makes them snowflakes is that approximately 20% to 80% of their quills are unbanded. Whites are similar in that the eyes and quills may be of any color, but fewer than 5% of their quills are banded. Similarly, pintos can have any color of quills and eyes, but possess patches or spots of unbanded quills with pink skin underneath. Albinos are those hedgehogs that have pink eyes, pink skin, and white quills- much like the appearance of an albino lab rat or mouse. If the eyes are not pink or there is

45

5f. The audience learns about hedgehogs while watching an IHA judge discuss hedgehog show entrants.

pigment to the skin, then the hedgehog is not an albino. The seventh color class, Any Other Color (AOC), is for those hedgehogs who do not meet the criteria for the other six classes. Examples of AOC colors would include double whites, who are not albino but have no banded quills, and confettis, who have a dot rather than a band on their quills.

It is important to note that hedgehog colors change quite a bit during a hedgehog's early life and you cannot tell with absolute certainty what a hedgehog's adult color will be when it is a baby. Patterns, such as snowflake and white, may not even begin to emerge until the hedgehog is 8 to 12 weeks old. Please see the section of this book on baby colors for more details about baby colors. In dark hedgehogs, you will also see age-related fading of skin and quill color. Approximately 12 to 18 months old is the optimal age for determining a hedgehog's phenotypic (expressed) color.

The hedgehog community

The International Hedgehog Association (IHA) was originally founded under the name International Hedgehog Fanciers Society (IHFS) on July 15, 1995. The name was changed to the International Hedgehog Club (IHC) in August of 1999, after a reorganization. The name was again changed to International Hedgehog Association (IHA) in 2001, to better reflect its mission. IHA is a registered charitable non-profit organization that was established to educate the public in the care and betterment of hedgehogs by facilitating rescue, welfare, promotion, and care of pet hedgehogs.

The International Hedgehog Association provides a wide range of services to the hedgehog community. IHA publishes a monthly newsletter called Hedgehog Central that serves to address hedgehog care issues of interest to beginners and advanced hedgehog fans alike. IHA maintains a network of experienced pet hedgehog rescue stations, to assist in the care, rehabilitation, and placement of pet hedgehogs who are displaced from their homes. The IHA maintains the International Hedgehog Registry, a central database where hedgehogs are registered in order to track lineages, health issues, longevity, and other information that is helpful in improving the quality of the species. The IHA maintains a network of breeder members and promotes ethical breeding practices. The IHA also promotes hedgehog shows as a means of bringing people together and educating persons about the care of pet hedgehogs. IHA also supports research activities that are helpful to the care of pet hedgehogs. Members are encouraged to join committees to become involved in the organization's activities and greater benefit hedgehogs and those who love them.

Showing your hedgehog

5g. Hedgehog show entrants are closely examined by the judge while at the show table.

The International Hedgehog Association (IHA) promotes hedgehog shows for the purpose of education, camaraderie, fun, and promotion of quality in breeding programs. These events typically include the actual show, where a trained judge talks about the animals as they work, discussing differences, explaining things about color, the IHA show standard, and highlighting those characteristics that make a hedgehog an ideal show (and pet) hedgehog.

The IHA show system itself promotes quality in breeding standards. Thirty-three percent of the 100 points allotted are for temperament while the rest of the points go for generally good flow, form, and coloration. The body style that is preferred, a teardrop shape that is not overly plump, has been correlated with greater longevity in preliminary studies. Shows give breeders the opportunity to talk with each other and share husbandry practices, learning new things to improve the care of their hedgehogs and quality of their lines.

Many hedgehog shows also include educational seminars and social events. The hedgehog community is quite wonderful in that the shows have evolved as a vehicle for education, rather than purely competition. Someone may go home with the grand prize, but everyone goes home with new information and new friendships. It is very reaffirming to see other hedgehog owners putting the same degree of dedication and passion into their prickly friends as you.

Online communities

As with most things in this day and age, a considerable community of hedgehog resources has developed on the Internet. Anyone browsing the Internet for hedgehog information should be aware that the quality of information varies from excellent to downright dangerous. All information should be evaluated with a good dose of common sense and double checked when possible. Online hedgehog communities appear to be of two basic types: bulletin boards, and mailing lists. A listing of several online resources that are currently active as of the printing of this book is available in the resources section of the appendix.

5h. Best of Show and Reserve Best of Show pose by their trophies and ribbons.

Bulletin boards, also called BBS, are places where there is usually a central page that list topic areas, then individual questions and comments, organized in "threads" (topic areas), can be posted. People respond to these posts and everything that is posted can be read and responded to by any members. These typically stay posted for a long period of time and anyone can browse the BBS to gain information. In order to post, most will require that you give basic information about yourself (typically kept private) and then you are assigned a profile name, a name uniquely yours that you choose to use on the BBS, that will identify all of your posts.

Mailing lists are lists where persons interested in the list's topic can sign up to receive all e-mails sent to the list. Most will give you the option of receiving all individual e-mails, a daily digest, or of accessing them on a central web location. A number of different hedgehog mailing lists exist today, each with a somewhat different focus. Some focus on health concerns, some on building human and even hedgehog friendships, and some more regionally oriented.

When using Internet forums such as a BBS or mailing list, it is important to observe proper netiquette. You must remember that you are there to learn more about hedgehogs and that the purpose of these lists is education. Individuals come to these lists with a wide variety of backgrounds and beliefs and may not share your views. Discussion should focus on resolving differences of opinion in a constructive manner that will help everyone to learn and better their knowledge and ability to care for their hedgehog companions.

Preparing for a pet sitter

There are times when one may need to travel and simply cannot take their hedgehog on the trip. It can be difficult to find a person who is experienced with hedgehogs to provide care in your absence, but taking time in advance can help even a first time hedge-sitter to provide care with confidence. The following items are things that you need to review with your pet sitter:
- specific information about your feeding program.
- a caution about environmental concerns, such as temperature, and a warning about hedgehog prowess at escape.
- a demonstration and practice with how to properly handle the hedgehog.
- the phone number where you can be reached.
- the name and phone number of your veterinarian and at least one other person who is knowledgeable about hedgehogs.
- a description of your hedgehog's typical behavior and what types of behavior would be reason to contact you, the veterinarian, or a knowledgeable hedgehog person.

By providing this information, your pet sitter will know what to feed your hedgehog, how to keep your hedgehog safe and happy, and should be able to manage basic problems. In addition, both you and the pet sitter will feel comfortable knowing that you are both prepared in case of emergency. It should be noted that some hedgehogs develop attachment to their owners, which becomes apparent by the hedgehog's reaction to the owner's absence. It may become overactive while its pattern is interrupted- dumping out the food dish, knocking over the wheel, and so on. It may also pout when you return, behaving in an extra prickly, grumpy manner when you get home. Soothing talk, feeding treats, and returning to the normal schedule helps your hedgehog get back on track when this occurs.

Chapter 6: Breeding hedgehogs

Introduction to the perils of breeding

One of the first things that many people think when they enjoy an animal companion is, "Gee, wouldn't it be nice to have babies." There are many well-intentioned reasons for this, but also many reasons why it is not a good idea. First, it may endanger the health of the female hedgehog. Pregnancy related problems, such as a ruptured uterus, can claim the mother's life. Further, c-sections in the event of complications can cost several hundred dollars and you still may not be able to save the babies.

Second, hedgehogs of unknown lineage may carry genetic problems that you do not want to pass off to their offspring. Sometimes these problems will not become apparent until the hedgehog is at the prime of breeding age and it is heartbreaking to watch one after another as parent and children all succumb to an inherited disease such as WHS. In addition, age is often unknown and breeding a female who is not in her prime breeding age creates considerable risk to her health.

Third, hedgehogs have a fairly high rate of infant mortality, with cannibalism as the primary cause. It is believed that hedgehogs are prone to cannibalism if they feel that there is any reason why their babies might not survive, such as less than optimal weather conditions (especially rapid changes in barometric pressure), the mother's health, disturbances to the mother, or health problems in the baby. Their natural environment is sufficiently harsh that it aids the mother's survival to make such seemingly brutal decisions. Approximately 1/3 of captive born hedgehog babies do not make it to weaning age, with most of these deaths occurring in the first 24 hours of life. The rate appears highest for first time mothers and mothers past the age of about 2 to 2-1/2. It may be especially disturbing for children in the family to observe the remains of a cannibalized litter.

Finally, it may be difficult to find homes for babies once they are born. If you are going to raise babies, you need to be prepared to provide a home for them in the event that they are not sold or that the home to which they are sold does not work out. If you live in the United States, you are required to have a USDA license in order to sell or even give away the babies.

Licensure

In the United States, a USDA license is currently required to sell or even give away hedgehogs and other exotic pocket pets. This is a national requirement and applies to persons anywhere in the US. The cost of this license, called a Class A license for breeders and a Class B license for brokers, is based on the amount of sales. The contact information for the USDA department that oversees this licensure can be found in the Appendix under resources. In order to obtain a USDA license, the animal facility (which may be your home) must meet the general specifications outlined in the Animal Welfare Act. You must complete a Plan of Veterinary Care (PVC) form with your veterinarian, who must visit your facility at least once a year for an inspection. Once you have completed these requirements, a USDA inspector will visit to ensure that you are in compliance with the requirements. Once you are licensed, you will receive inspections at least once a year on a surprise basis. Some states, counties, and cities will have their own licensure requirements that must be met in addition to the USDA licensure. Penalties for ignoring licensure requirements can include warnings, fines, confiscation of animals, and jail time.

6a. Five-day-old hedgehog babies.

The many hats of a hedgehog breeder

In addition to being prepared to handle the potential problems that inevitably arise, being a successful hedgehog breeder means handling more tasks than just putting two animals together. . Putting two animals of breeding age together is the easiest part- the rest isn't as simple. Here are some of the hats that you will need to learn to wear if you decide that you want to raise hedgehogs:

1. <u>Sanitation engineer</u>: If you're going to raise animals, you're going to have to scoop poop. Hedgehogs require cage cleaning at least once a week, or more, depending on the type of bedding that you choose to use. This can be quite time consuming if you have many hedgehogs. With 50 hedgehogs, I spend roughly 8 hours cleaning cages every weekend.

2. <u>Behaviorist</u>: You have to get to know your animals and become familiar with their normal routines so that you will know when things are okay and when things are not right. You will need to learn how to work with animals who are not easily handled and how to bring out their best. You will need to be prepared to help others learn to do the same. If you want your customers to be happy, you will need to know how to help them solve common behavior problems- whether that means intervening with the customer's expectations or helping them to implement behavior modification for the animal.

6b. Three-week-old hedgehog baby.

3. <u>Vet tech</u>: You will need to learn to handle basic medical problems. The more animals you have, the more opportunities for things to go wrong. Hedgehogs always seem to get sick late Friday night on 3 day weekends so it's really important to know what to do until you can get a hold of the veterinarian. You also need to be able to identify potential problems. Nobody can detect all problems, but you will need to be able to demonstrate to your customers that you are able to take reasonable care. If your customer's hedgehog has problems later down the road, you will be the first person they ask for help, so you need to be prepared to help them with their questions.

4. <u>Legal beagle</u>: You need to know what laws govern hedgehog sales where you live, as well as an awareness of laws that apply to persons to whom you are selling. Local, state or province, and federal laws may apply. They are prone to changing at the drop of a hat. If you ship out of state, you need to know where NOT to send a hedgehog. Just because they're legal for you doesn't mean you're not responsible for trying to send them places where they've been banned, or letting your customers figure that out for themselves by running afoul of the law. You also need to be very aware of your sales policies and provide a very clear statement of what constitutes your responsibility and the buyer's responsibility to all potential customers.

5. <u>Marketing expert</u>: Hedgehogs don't just sell themselves, especially if people don't know that you have them for sale. First, you have to figure out a way to reach potential customers. Then you need to convince them that they should buy from you. There are lots of hedgehog breeders out there and some complain that they can't hardly give them away, while others enjoy reasonably steady business. You aren't just selling an animal, you're selling your expertise and quality. You need to be able to instill confidence that you can provide these things and to follow through. After all, one happy customer may send one more your way. And one unhappy customer will tell 100 not to do business with you. You can't please everybody, but it sure helps if you try your best.

6. <u>Travel agent</u>: Most breeders find that the local market for hedgehogs is not very big and shipping becomes a necessity. Air freight or licensed van lines are the only legal way to ship mammals and that can mean dealing with the airlines. Shipping regulations can change frequently and what may be the rule one day may be different the next. You will earn lots of gray hairs during this part of the process.

7. <u>Public relations/education</u>: You have to like people, not just hedgehogs. If you enjoy working with your customers, helping them to become better educated and answering all their questions, they will enjoy working with you. They will also have a much better relationship with their hedgehog because they will be better prepared and will have a more realistic idea of what to expect. If you do not enjoy working with people and

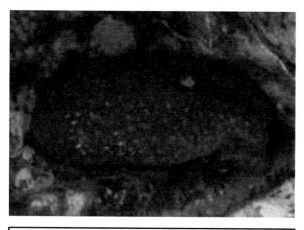

6c. Newborn hedgehog baby.

answering lots of questions, you will quickly become frustrated with this part of the process.

8. <u>Banker</u>: You will have start up costs for your hedgehogs and for equipment. You will need to track income and expenditures for tax purposes. You will need to be able to budget for the cost of quality food, bedding, and so on. Your utility bills may increase to meet the temperature needs of your hedgehogs. There will be animal losses, damaged equipment, phone bills to customers, advertising, veterinary bills, and so on. Not all breeders produce, and you will need to budget for the care of your nonproducing animals.

9. <u>Emergency services provider</u>: You will need to be prepared to handle emergencies. This includes emergencies for the hedgehogs, as well as environmental emergencies. What if the power goes out? What if there is a flood? A fire? A tornado? You have to be prepared to respond to take full care and responsibility for your animals under any conditions.

10. <u>Rescue worker</u>: If you are involved in breeding, you will need to be involve in rescue. Once word gets out that you have hedgehogs, sick or displaced hedgehogs will somehow find their way to your door.

I'm sure there are plenty more hats to wear, but those are the ones that first come to mind. If you enjoy your critters, enjoy learning, think creatively, and like to work with people, you've got the beginnings of what it takes. I strongly recommend that people gain at least a year to two of experience owning hedgehogs before trying to breed them. It's hard to fill these hats without a strong base of knowledge and experience to go along with the basics.

Breeder ethics
The International Hedgehog Association has established a Code of Breeder Ethics that serves as a guideline to help breeders understand what is needed to provide quality care to both animals and customers. Breeding should not be undertaken casually, rather it should reflect care to improve the quality of the species. Items covered in this code include:
- only breeding and selling hedgehogs that are healthy and not known to carry any health problem suspected of being genetically linked.
- participating in registration with the International Hedgehog Registry and keeping records that assist in furthering an understanding of hedgehog health and lifespan issues.
- obtaining and maintaining all appropriate licensure.

6d. Week-old babies nursing. This mother hedgehog chose a hedgebag for nesting.

- a commitment to educating people about hedgehogs before purchase.
- to have experience in the care of pet hedgehogs prior to undertaking any breeding program.
- provide a written copy of all policies and guarantees to all customers.
- provide proper food, water, and environment for your hedgehogs.
- not allowing babies to leave your care until they are fully weaned.
- refusal to sell animals to persons in places where the animal would be in danger due to legal status of hedgehogs in the locale.
- a commitment to furthering your own knowledge of hedgehog care and to working with an experienced mentor as you begin your breeding program.

From beginning to babies
If you have taken all of these considerations in mind, have spent some time learning about pet hedgehogs through ownership of your own pets, have a good working relationship with your veterinarian, have obtained any required licensure, and have found an appropriate mentor, you are ready to begin.

Choosing breeding stock
There are many important things to consider when choosing breeding stock. Keeping in mind that the purpose is breeding is not simply to produce babies, but to produce quality, friendly babies, hedgehogs who are chosen for breeding should be healthy and have a family history that is known to be free from problems that are suspected of being genetically linked. Purchasing breeding stock who are registered with the International Hedgehog Registry (IHR) and checking the family tree will allow you to determine whether there are issues in an individual hedgehog's background that would make it unsuitable for breeding. If you choose to breed a hedgehog that is not registered, please register that hedgehog so that the information is available to future generations. Hedgehogs who have any immediate health problems should not be bred until that problem is resolved and it is certain that breeding will not pose a risk to the hedgehog.

The hedgehog's age should also be a consideration. Although hedgehogs are able to reproduce at a very early age, they are not considered completely physically mature until they are 5 to 6 months of age. For females, age is especially important. The optimal age for a female's first litter seems to be about 6 months to 1 year of age. The optimal breeding period for females seems to end somewhere around age 2 to 3, marked by decreased conceptions, increased abandonment of litters, and pregnancy complications. Many males will reproduce throughout their entire life span.

6e. Newborn hedgehogs do not have quills poking through. The quills begin to emerge in the first hour.

Temperament is also an important consideration. Because much of a hedgehog's temperament is inherited, you want to choose hedgehogs with a friendly demeanor. Hedgehogs who are aggressive or excessively shy should not be bred.

Color may also be a consideration. Please keep in mind that hedgehogs are not necessarily a "what you see is what you get" species as far as color goes. Breeding two hedgehogs of a color that you like increases the chances that you will get similarly colored babies, but the parents may also carry additional color genes that they can contribute to the babies. Knowing several generations of the colors in the family tree helps with predicting the color of offspring that they can produce.

Putting them together

Before you put your male and female together you will need to have a clean cage set up, with sufficient space for them to court. Be sure to observe them for at least the first 15 minutes to an hour and be within earshot for the first several hours so that you can separate them if aggression occurs. Typically, the male will begin to "sing" at the female, who may huffle and run away. If she is receptive, she will flatten out and allow him to mount her. This can happen very quickly or may take several days for her to decide to cooperate. Most breeders will leave their male and female together for approximately 1 week before moving the female to her pregnancy suite.

Pregnancy

The female must be kept separate from the male during her pregnancy because they will most likely eat the babies if they are together when the babies are born. The mother's pregnancy suite should include a hiding place where she can build her nest when her time comes closer. Some females arrange very elaborate nest areas, while others do little in the way of preparation. Gestation is typically 35 to 40 days after first introduction to the male. If babies are not born by 40 days after the last day with the male, she is most likely not pregnant.

Females generally do not need any extra supplements during their pregnancy. Be sure to provide plenty of her usual food and treats, and consult the veterinarian if you have any concerns about her health or nutrition. Care should be taken to minimize stressors, such as noise, during the pregnancy. At approximately 32 days after her first introduction to the male, you should give the cage a very thorough cleaning in preparation for the babies' arrival.

6f. At two weeks old, this baby is very large, but the eyes are still closed.

Most females will have gained at least 40 grams by the time they reach the 30th day of pregnancy, so careful attention to weight gain is a useful clue. However, it is not foolproof. Some females appear to go through false pregnancies and gain weight, but there are no babies. Some hedgehogs gain little to no weight and have large litters. It is also believed that hedgehogs can reabsorb babies. Presumably this serves their survival in the wild, but can create infections and birthing problems. Often times, females who are close to birthing will have nipples that become somewhat enlarged for nursing. The belly may become tight and hard, and you may be able to actually feel the outline of the babies. However, the only entirely certain way to tell whether a female is pregnant is via ultrasound or x-ray as some females who are pregnant give no visible signs to let you predict their condition.

It is common for females to begin hiding in their nest for two to three days prior to birthing their babies. She may go off of her feed for a day or two. When labor begins, the female will usually become extremely active, giving the appearance that she is going berserk. You will need to make sure that her cage is in a quiet, private place and you should take care not to disturb her during this time unless there is reason to believe that something has gone wrong. If it appears that something has gone wrong, call the veterinarian immediately and be ready to describe exactly what is going on so that the veterinarian can help you determine what to do next.

Infancy It is very important to leave the mother hedgehog alone after her babies are born. You will want to give a visual check to the cage to make sure that there are no deceased babies in the cage. If you find any, they will need to be removed. If you see that there are any babies who are not in the nest, give the mother a few hours to collect them and bring them into the nest before you attempt to place them back with her. This should be the only reason to intrude upon a mother hedgehog and any intrusion should be kept to the bare minimum. If you want to know for sure if she has babies, listen very carefully for the sound of suckling or the peeping of babies.

Mother hedgehogs will sometimes become nervous and engage in the disturbing behavior of carrying their babies around the cage, seeming to look for a place to put the babies. This behavior can be very upsetting to the hedgehog owner, especially as the baby squeals in protest. Unless she is hurting the babies, you should not intervene. If she is running in a wheel with the babies, you will want to remove the wheel until the babies are a little older. If you can quietly place a treat in mother's food dish, this will sometimes distract her interest from carrying the baby around. Offering an additional hide place may also calm her down, as she relocates her baby to the place that she feels most comfortable. If she is injuring the babies, you will need to decide whether they are in enough danger to warrant removing them for hand rearing. Hand rearing is risky, so should only be considered if you think that the babies are at risk of serious injury or death.

6g. At three weeks old, babies are still nursing though they start to look like miniature adults.

Until the babies are 2 to 3 weeks old, you will want to minimize interruptions. Do not attempt to peek in the nest and definitely do not try to clean the entire cage. You will want to spot clean the messiest areas of the cage, scooping out soiled bedding to replace with clean, but you must take care not to disturb the nest. The mother's behavior is your best clue as to how much intrusion is acceptable. If she huffles and charges your hand, you can be certain that she does not want you near her babies.

Hedgehog babies are born with no quills poking out. They have pink skin and a thin membrane over the quill area. When they are born, the mother will lick them to remove the membrane and stimulate breathing before she moves them into the nest. Within an hour, tiny white quills begin to poke through the skin. By 24 hours, babies that will have pigmented skin and noses will begin to show coloration in these areas. By the end of a week, they should have some banded quills, although quill color in infancy is not necessarily the color that the hedgehog will exhibit as an adult. They may peep if they are hungry or cannot find their mother. Babies are considered infants until approximately 3 weeks old, at which point they should have their eyes open, teeth coming in, and look like miniature adults who are unsteady on their feet.

Toddlerhood

When hedgehog babies move into toddlerhood, their mothers will typically become less defensive about letting you near them. By the time they are 3 weeks old, you can generally remove mother and babies to a separate enclosure and give the cage a thorough cleaning. Babies at this age are very curious and may lick your hands and anoint themselves. By three to four weeks, they should begin to try solid foods on their own. They may follow mother around the cage and she may even seem to be showing them the ropes of how to use the water bottle and find the food dish. Nursing will still be their primary source of food at this age, so they should not be away from the mother for more than an hour at a time.

6h. At four weeks old, the babies are beginning to eat solid food and explore, but still sleep in the nest, snuggled with mom and siblings.

By the time babies are approximately four weeks old, you should be prepared to register them with the International Hedgehog Registry. This allows the Registry time to complete the litter registration coupons and return them to you before your babies leave your home. Registering your babies allows the registry to track hedgehog births and allows persons who receive your babies to easily obtain any available records of their lineage. It also allows us to learn more about hedgehog breeding and babies through the accumulation of information in the database. Even if you have a litter where no babies survive, you should report this information to the IHR. There is a small fee for obtaining litter registration certificates, but they allow the hedgehog's new owner to complete the registration at no additional cost.

Weaning

Most baby hedgehogs will begin to wean themselves onto hard foods by about 5 weeks of age. At this point, they look like small adults and are steady on their feet. Before a baby is ready to be sold, you should observe that it has been eating and drinking on its own for at least one week and does not appear to be nursing. Most babies reach this milestone by 6 to 7 weeks old. Baby males should not be kept with their mothers and sisters after about 7 weeks old, to decrease the chance of accidental inbreeding. There are cases on record of females becoming pregnant at as young as 7 weeks and males who have impregnated their mothers when as young as 5-1/2 weeks. Typically, separating males from females at 6 to 7 weeks old is sufficient to avoid most unplanned pregnancies. It should be noted that males will often tolerate the presence of another male litter mate for several weeks after weaning, but you should be prepared to separate them by the time they are 12 weeks old, or in the event of any potentially aggressive behavior.

Hand feeding

When raising hedgehogs, there are times when it becomes necessary to hand feed the babies. This should only occur in situations where the mother neglects or injures the babies, or becomes too sick to care for the babies. Hand feeding does not improve the babies' temperament, and is too risky to undertake unless baby's life is already endangered. Many hand fed babies do not survive, despite the best efforts of the caretaker, so hand feeding should only be done as a last resort.

If a situation does arise where a mother is not able to care for her baby, I use a shoe box sized container with soft cloth for bedding. A heating pad on low is placed under half of the box, so that the baby can get closer or further from it as needed. It is very important to have the extra heat source, since baby animals cannot produce their own heat. The baby also needs to be able to move closer and further from the heat so that it does not become overheated.

You should never give a baby hedgehog cow's milk as the baby is not equipped to digest the lactose. Puppy milk replacer and goat's milk are the most frequently used milk replacers for hand feeding hedgehogs and are reported to be much more successful than kitten replacer. You should not use human infant formula or ensure as these are not appropriate. You can obtain a 1 cc syringe with a plastic end and no needle from your veterinarian or pharmacist to use as a
 device. An eyedropper can work, but the syringe allows more control over the rate of the milk. I will usually hold the baby in one hand so that the face is sticking out over my thumb and the body is enclosed in my hand. I put the syringe to the baby's lips and let just a little bit out. If the baby does not start to suckle, I gently use the syringe to open the baby's mouth and let a few drops at a time go in, giving baby time to swallow before giving more.

It seems like the babies have very different amounts that they want or will accept. Remember that tiny babies have tiny tummies, and overfeeding will be just as fatal as not feeding. More small feedings are better than one huge feeding. For very young babies, approximately two to three mouth fulls per feeding, given every two hours, is a good rate to start with. Babies who are hungry will generally start to peep, to let you know that they want more. As they get older, they will be able to eat more and will be able to have their feeding times further apart.

Stimulating the baby's digestive system after feedings is extremely important. Moms usually lick their babies' bellies to help get the digestive tract going. This is simulated by rubbing gently from chin to rectum with something like a damp cotton swab or cotton ball. There isn't any "magic number" of times to do this. I have done about 20 to 30 strokes after each feeding and that seems to have worked out fine. You'll know the baby's digestive system isn't working well if the belly becomes blackened in color and/or hard. When you give hedgehog babies anything other than mom's milk, they get green stools. Sometimes it is really shockingly green, so don't be alarmed. As they get weaned on to hard foods, the stools will become a more normal color.

6i. Three-week old hedgehog babies start to explore!

The babies will start to get teeth when they are about 3 weeks old. Start offering some ground up dry food that's been moistened with warm water in a low jar lid so they have the opportunity to feed themselves between hand feedings. They may anoint with it at first, but keep offering it. Once they are eating the moistened food, you can then switch to ground up dry, and then whole dry food. They should be able to handle adult food by the time they are five to six weeks old.

Predicting adult color from baby color

All hedgehog babies are born pink and without quills. Within about an hour, little white quills begin to emerge from under the skin. In the following day or so, if they are going to be a darker hedgehog, they begin to get some pigment to the skin and quills with pigmented bands grow in. Sometimes these banded quills have really odd shades of gray or tan that are not seen in adults. At about two to three weeks, they go through a quilling process and get a second set of baby spines that may be another different shade. The adult quills usually start to emerge when baby is about six to eight weeks old. A hedgehog that will be a white or snowflake usually looks just like any other solid color hedgehog until this process begins.

By about three weeks old, the eyes open. If the hedgehog is Algerian or in the darker color range, then the eyes will look black. If the hedgehog is going to be in the lighter color range, then its eyes will look red. An albino will have pink eyes. Sometimes eyes can look garnet colored at three weeks old, but may darken to black by eight weeks old. The skin and nose may also slightly darken in pigment and a baby that is very, very dark and has black spines at 3 weeks may lighten slightly in skin pigment and grow in slightly lighter bands during this time.

With all these changes going on, sometimes it seems like baby changes from day to day or week to week. It can be really fun or really frustrating when trying to guess what the final color will be! One thing that you usually can tell all along is whether the baby will be a pinto, if it has pigmented skin. This is because the areas where the white quills will grow in have only pink skin underneath. Sometimes the areas grow smaller as hedgehog grows larger, but you can tell where the spots will be! Most babies finish changing by the time they are about 12 to 16 weeks old. Occasionally, hedgehogs will turn white or snowflake at up to about six moths old, but for the most part, you only have to wait the three to four months to see the final color.

6j. Six-week old babies that are weaned and ready to be separated from mom and siblings.

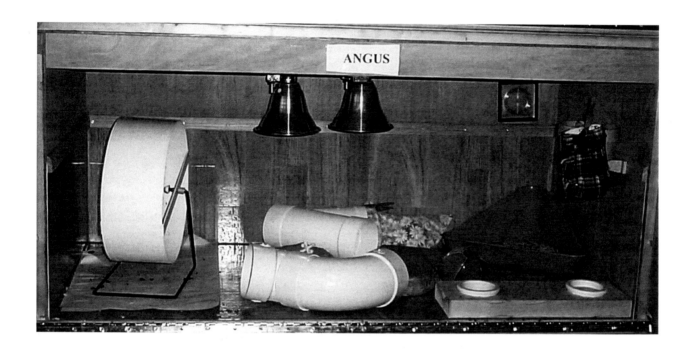

A home made wooden habitat, photo courtesy of Penelope McQuarrie. The front on this habitat is made of plexiglass, for easy visibility. Note the lamps that are included for warmth. A red bulb can be used at night to provide warmth without brightness. Hedgehogs do not seem to see the red light, so that is a good way to be able to watch them while they go about their nightly activity! Also note the litter box. Some hedgehogs readily adapt to litter box training, while others do not.

Chapter 7: Making things for your hedgehog

Hedgebag
A hedgebag is a sort of "sleeping bag" for hedgehogs, made of two pieces of cloth that are sewn into bags, then one tucked into the other and stitched down to enclose close edges and create a cozy place for hedgehog to hide. Fabrics to be used for hedgebags should be tightly woven and all loose edges must be enclosed as some hedgehogs will dig and you do not want loose threads to get wrapped around the hedgehog's limbs. Tightly woven cotton or cotton blend fabrics are recommended because they breathes enough to be cool in the summer, but helps hold in body heat and keep the hedgehog warm in the winter. Sometimes these bags are made with fleece, but if you use wood shavings, the shavings will stick to the fleece and become quite messy.

Craft foam tubes Many hedgehogs love to play with toilet paper tubes. They often wear them on their heads like a tank and strut about. In order to make sturdier tubes, you can measure a piece of craft foam to fit around a toilet paper tube, leaving about ½" extra space for overlap. Use nontoxic glue from a glue gun to glue it down at the overlap, allow to dry, and give to hedgehog for play! Occasionally, a hedgehog will try to eat the tube. If this happens, then it should be removed from the cage.

Storage tote cage

Large clear plastic storage bins make a wonderful light-weight, easy to clean hedgehog cages. They are inexpensive and can be purchased at many home improvement or discount stores. When purchasing the storage bin, you should make sure that it is a color that will allow light to come through and the floor space should provide at least three square feet of room. To turn the bin into a cage, you can use a drill or sautering iron to create holes for attaching the water bottle. It needs to be attached from the outside, with the water bottle spout pointing into the cage at approximately hedgehog shoulder height. Attaching from the outside prevents the hedgehog from using the water bottle to shinny out of the cage. If you must put the lid on the cage, use a ½" drill bit to drill ventilation holes. There should be enough holes to allow the hedgehog to breathe easily and to prevent condensation from occurring in the cage.

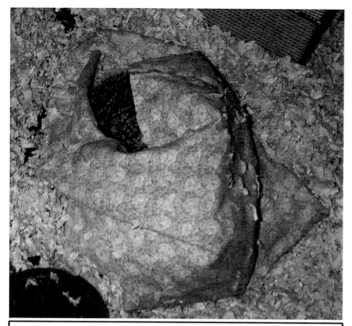

7a. This hedgehog is snug and cozy in her hedgebag. Hedgehogs need a place to hide and feel safe.

7b. A typical storage tote cage. Note that the ventilation holes are up high to prevent the hedgehog from kicking shavings out of the cage. The water bottle is mounted on the outside to reduce the likelihood of escape.

Fleece blanket

Polar fleece can make a very nice, simple, comfortable blanket for your hedgehog. Simply cut the polar fleece into a square of approximately 12" x 12" and provide it to your hedgehog for snuggling. There are a very few hedgehogs who will chew on polar fleece, creating a danger of intestinal blockage. If you notice your hedgehog chewing on the polar fleece, it should be removed.

Storage blocks playpen

Storage blocks can be purchased from a variety of office supply and discount stores. These consist of a variety of square grids that can be connected with plastic knobs at the corners. These can be reconfigured to make a playpen of the shape and proportions that you desire. A hedgehog should not be left alone in any configuration that does not include a secure floor and ceiling as they can squeeze under or climb out.

Toys from "trash"

Hedgehogs enjoy many simple treasures that are made from things we might ordinarily throw away. They will often enjoy playing with toilet paper tubes, as mentioned in the section on making foam tubes. They also tend to enjoy small boxes to climb in and on. They seem to enjoy squeezing into cereal boxes, in particular. Some hedgehogs seem to enjoy rustling around in old tissue paper, though colored papers should be avoided in case the hedgehog chooses to self-anoint. Old oatmeal containers make great hide boxes. Just use your imagination, think ahead and avoid potential dangers, and let your creativity be the guide!

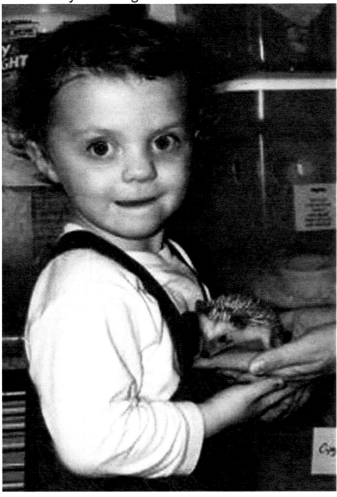

7c. A young hedgehog enthusiast.

7d. A home made wheel, made from a cake pan and plastic storage box. Photo courtesy of Penelope McQuarrie.

7e. A hedgehog playing "Tank Boy" with his craft foam tube. Photo courtesy of Penelope McQuarrie.

Chapter 8: Resources

Bibliography
Graffam, Wendy (1998). http://www.gohogwild.net/ghw98/nutrition.htm
Hoefer Heidi (1994). Hedgehogs. Vet Clin North America: Small Animal Practice, 24(1),113-120.
Johnston, Jeff (1999). University of North Carolina, Chapel Hill, http://www.trifl.org/cedar.html

Recommended Readings
Hedgehog Central. monthly publication of the International Hedgehog Society. Available by subscription for $20 per year. Http://hedgehogclub.com or IHA, PO Box 1060, Divide, CO 80814.
Larsden, R. Scott DVM and Carpenter, James W DVM (1999). Husbandry and medical management of African Hedgehogs. Veterinary Medicine, 94 (10), 877-888.
Massena, Sharon and Smith, Bryan. The Pygmy Hedgehog: A Perfect Pet.
Sykes, Lenny and Durant, Jane. The Natural Hedgehog, Gaia Press.
Wrobel, Dawn and Brown, Dr. Susan (1997). The Hedgehog: An Owner's Guide to a Happy, Healthy Pet, John Wiley and Sons, Inc.

Internet Resources

<u>General Information</u>
Hedgehog Central: http://hedgehogcentral.com
Hedgehog Valley: http://hedgehogvalley.com
Pogstar Hedgehogs: http://www.pogstarhedgehogs.com
Pets Hub: http://petshub.com/hedgehogs/
Welsh Hedgehog Hospital: http://www.whh.org

Organizations
International Hedgehog Association: http://hedgehogclub.com or or IHA, PO Box 1060, Divide, CO 80814.
International Hedgehog Registry: http://hedgehogregistry.org or IHR, PO Box 122, Yates Center, KS 66749.

Hedgehogabilia
Hedgehog Valley at Café Press: http://www.cafeshops.com/hhvalley
Daisy Meadows Hedgehogs: http://hedgehogaholica.tripod.com/hedgehogaholica/catalog
Critter Connection: http://www.critterconnection.cc/index.htm
Hedgehog Books: http://www.hedgehogbooks.com/
Hedgehog Gear: http://www.hedgehoggear.com/
Hedgehog Supplies at The Ferret Store: http://www.ferretstore.com/hedgehogs.html
Pins-N-Needles: http://www.pins-n-needles.net (source for Arata liners)
Massena's Menagerie: http://www.massena.com/sharon
Rubber Hedgehog: http://www.rubberhedgehog.com/
Kritters In The Mailbox: http://www.krittersinthemailbox.com

Mailing lists and BBSs:
Go to http://groups.yahoo.com and search for hedgehog_help (care issues) or hedgehog world (hedgehog community).
Chin-n-Quills: http://www.chins-n-quills.com
EOTC Pets Forum: http://www.eotc-pets.com/forums/index.php
Paw-Talk Pet Forum: http://www.paw-talk.net

Veterinary Care Issues:
Common Hedgehog Disorders: http://www.mihog.org/disorders.phtml
Health Articles at Hedgehog Valley: http://hedgehogvalley.com/vethealth.html
Health Articles at Hedgies.com: http://www.hedgies.com/hedgehog_health_care.htm
Hedgehog Health: http://www.animalhospitals-usa.com/small_pets/hedgehog_health.html
Hedgehog Nutrition Information: http://www.gohogwild.net/ghw98/nutrition.htm
Michigan Vet Conference Proceedings: http://www.hillary.net/hedgehog.txt
Veterinary Care for Hedgehogs Lecture: http://www.gohogwild.net/ghw98/vetcare.htm
Veterinarian List: http://hedgehogcentral.com/care/vets.html

Hedgehog Food:
Mazuri Insectivore Diet: http://www.buymazuri.net/
Spike's Delite: http://antigonemeans.tripod.com/spike.html
8 in 1 Hedgehog Food: http://www.ferretstore.com/h-457.html
Zoo Fare Insectivore Fare: http://sugarglider.safeshopper.com/65/cat65.htm?938
Select Diet: http://www.massena.com/sharon/hhcatalog.htm

8a. A male hedgehog.

8b. Setifer Setosus, or the Greater Madagascar Hedgehog Tenrec, is also an insectivore with quills. Notice that their feet are extremely different from an African hedgehog's.

A female hedgehog

Chapter 9: Index

Adjustment 22, 23
Appetite 15, 24, 32, 36, 38
Arata liner 17, 66
Bath 18, 40, 41
Bedding 3, 6, 9, 16-18, 21, 23, 34, 35, 42, 51, 53, 57, 58
Biting 44, 28, 27
Breeder ethics 53
Breeding 4, 5, 43, 46, 47, 50, 51, 53-55, 58
Cage 2, 3, 6, 11-15, 17, 18, 24, 25, 27, 29, 37, 39, 42, 43, 51, 55-57, 63
Cancer 6, 33, 36
Color 5, 17, 20, 45-47, 55, 57, 59, 60
Dental 15, 32, 36, 37
Escape 11-13, 15, 16, 29, 30, 44
Eyes 8, 32, 35, 45, 46, 57, 60
Feet 9, 11, 40, 41, 57, 58
Feeding 5, 14, 15, 23, 36, 37, 43, 48, 49
Fleas 34, 39
Gender 5, 6, 20, 26

Hand Feeding 58, 59
Handling 3, 5, 8, 19, 20, 21, 22, 23, 25, 27, 28, 51
Hedgebag 18, 42, 62
Housing 11, 12
IHA (International Hedgehog Association) 46, 47, 66, 67
IHR (International Hedgehog Registry) 54, 67
Infection 9, 13, 15, 20, 32-38, 56
Mites 9, 18, 20, 33, 34, 35, 37
Nutrition 9, 14, 33, 39, 55, 66, 67
Obesity 3, 36, 37
Online communities 47
Personality 4, 6, 8, 20
Pet Sitter 48, 49
Pregnancy 50, 54-56
Quilling 3, 4, 19, 27, 28, 33, 60
Respiratory 13, 20, 32. 35, 36
Safety 15-17
Self-anointing 27-29, 40, 57, 59, 64
Shows 46, 47
Temperament 2, 4-6, 8, 13, 44, 47, 55, 58
Toys 18, 64
Travel 42, 48, 52
USDA licensure 2, 4, 5, 51
Weaning 50, 58, 59
Wobbly 32, 38, 39

Chapter 10: Appendices

Hedgehog's Journal

This section is meant as a place where you can store information about your hedgehog's background and health information. If you ever have to take your hedgehog to the veterinarian, you should take this with you as it will help the veterinarian understand your hedgehog's background and typical behavior.

Hedgehog's name:

Date of birth (or date obtained and estimate of birth date):

Where hedgehog was obtained:

Hedgehog's parents' names and where they came from:

Hedgehog's International Hedgehog Registry number:

What does hedgehog eat:

How much does hedgehog usually eat?

What kind of bedding does hedgehog sleep on:

What is hedgehog's sleep schedule?

Describe the furnishings in hedgehog's cage:

Dates hedgehog's nails are trimmed:

Dates and dispositions of any veterinary visits hedgehog has had:

Any medications hedgehog has been given:

Dates and descriptions of any unusual occurrences:
(in this section, include odd behaviors, changes in stool quality, or anything else that might suggest any health issues)

Date and weight on weigh-ins:

Additional Photos

Hedgehogs show up in the strangest places…

Hedgehog at the Beach and Hedgehog in the Snow art and photos courtesy of Penelope McQuarrie.

Weighing your hedgehog regularly helps you recognize weight loss, a symptom of many types of illness, so that you can seek treatment early.

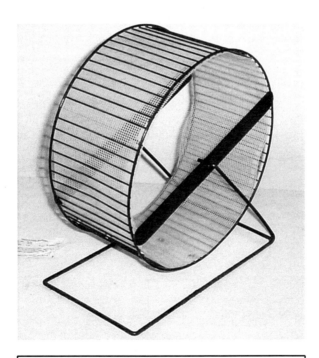

A wheel with wire spokes can be lined to make it safe for a hedgehog. Photo courtesy of Penelope McQuarrie.

Ways to say "hedgehog" in other languages:

Aafrikans: Krimpvarkie

French: Herisson

German: Igel

Bengali: kata Chua

Arabic: qunfud

Chinese: ci-wei

Danish: PINDSVIN

Czech: jezek

Finnish: Siili

Dutch: Egel

Hebrew: Kipod

Irish: Grainneog

Latin: Erinaceus

Italian: riccio

Japanese: HARINEZUMI

Maltese: Qanfud

Norwegian: piggsvin

Persian: kharpusht

Portugese: ourico

Russian: EZH

Punjabi: kanderala

Spanish: erizo

Swedish: igelkott

Welsh: draenog

Acknowledgements

I would like to thank all of the wonderful people who made this book possible. First I need to thank Gail Dick, whose gentle prompting ("Tig, you have to write a book.") got me going. Next, I need to thank those who gave me editorial help and/or reviewed the manuscript: Becca Loane, Nancy Adams, Penelope and Dr. Allan McQuarrie, Jane Lee, Debbie Burk, Gail Dick, and Darrell Monfort, DVM. I must thank my family for humoring me in with my hedgehog hobby and encouraging this book. My husband, Lance Burleson, has been a big support and our children, Persephone and Zury are the most wonderful hedgehog helpers I could ask for. I want to thank Penelope McQuarrie and Becca Loane for allowing me to use their photographs in this text (their photo credits appear directly below the photos they contributed). I want to thank the two people who mentored me most when I was a fresh, faced, question asking newbie to the hedgehog world- Bryan Smith and Sharon Massena. Their patience and encouragement helped me build the foundation up which my knowledge and experience has grown. I must also offer my thanks to those people who participate actively in the hedgehog community. It is only because of the efforts to share and disseminate information that we have come so long in such a short way, to the benefit of our hedgehog friends. I would especially like to thank everyone who is involved with the International Hedgehog Association, for their commitment to the welfare of and education about hedgehogs, and to anyone who has ever been dedicated enough put on a hedgehog show.

Visit our website:

http://hedgehogvalley.com

Every care has been taken to ensure that the information in this book is correct. No liability can be accepted by the authors or publishers for loss, damage, or injury caused by errors in, or omissions from, the information given. This information in this book is not meant to substitute for your veterinarian, it is to help you work with your veterinarian.